Stewardship Economy   6

property rights

Julian Pratt

Published by

Lulu.com

Editorial note

This book brings together previously unpublished material which
Julian worked on alongside the summary book, *Stewardship
Economy 1: private property without private ownership*. With the
other five books in the series, it provides the additional material
that lies behind the proposals and assertions made in book 1.
Unfortunately, aspects of this work are unfinished, some of the
examples provided are out of date, there is some repetition of text
and some references (bibliography in book 7) are not available. I
hope you, the reader, will excuse this and will find the work as a
whole thought-provoking and topical.

Rosemary Field

September 2021

ISBN 978-1-4717-0176-4

Contents

Books in the series

Stewardship Economy 1: private property without private ownership is the first book and provides an overall summary of the main ideas.

Stewardship Economy 2: Valuing land and managing transition sets out in some detail how to establish the market rent of land and how to make the transition from an ownership to a stewardship economy. It also considers how the revenue from stewardship fees might be distributed.

Stewardship Economy 3: Land, environment and climate (this book) explores how a stewardship economy would transform the way we use land, provide housing and develop our cities. It goes on to consider how stewardship would help address pressing environmental and climate concerns.

Stewardship Economy 4: The economy, wealth and universal income focuses on the impact of stewardship on the national and global economy, how the distribution of wealth would be changed and the impact of a Universal Income.

Stewardship Economy 5: efficient, fair taxes and the role of the state describes the some of the adverse effects of our current system of taxation and considers the role of the state in a stewardship economy. It also explains some basic economic principles and terms.

Stewardship Economy 6: property rights (this book) describes the systems of property rights in our current economic system, their history and how property rights could be more fair and efficient in a stewardship economy.

Stewardship Economy 7: some economics explained, economic terms and bibliography. This book provides an introduction to some key economic concepts for the non-specialist and lists the references, as far as they are available.

Introduction

This book, *Stewardship Economy 6: property rights,* explores the ethical basis of property rights with a particular emphasis on issues of fairness.

Chapter 1 establishes a language for thinking about property rights in an ownership economy and provides options for allocation of property rights in a stewardship economy, using the models of property rights applied in an ownership economy. The next five chapters encourage the reader to question the way we mostly accept as a 'given' the ownership of the natural world.

Chapter 2 then goes back a thousand years or so to follow the history of private property in England, including its origins in the feudal system and obligations to the Crown.

Chapter 3 explores the ethical basis for the ownership of private property and concludes that traditional justifications provide an equally sound ethical basis for stewardship.

Chapter 4 considers the arguments that have been advanced in favour of common property and discusses the obligations which were in the past an integral part of ownership but have been eroded.

Chapter 5 reminds us that land ownership almost always originates in the exercise of force and power.

Chapter 6 notes that economists have generally considered land and artefacts in the same category but recognises that this is changing.

Chapter 7 summarises the reasons why stewardship is a more ethical form of private property rights than our current arrangement.

Chapter 1 Systems of property rights and stewardship economy

This chapter introduces the four main systems of land tenure that have been recognised since the Roman era: open access regimes, private property, collective property and common property. These property systems are distinguished by asking 'who decides how the property is used?' This brief overview provides for a range of options for allocation of property rights in a stewardship economy.

Systems of property rights

'Land tenure' refers to the whole collection of laws, customs and practices governing the rights, duties and relationships of people to the land. At the core of any system of land tenure is a system of property rights, the purpose of which is to resolve problems of the allocation of property. It consists of a set of rules governing access to, and control of, the natural world and artefacts.

While property systems may, from within a particular society, appear to be fixed and unchangeable, they vary considerably between societies and at different times. Choosing to accept the status quo is as much a choice as is challenging it. Richard Schlatter noted in 1951 that the question of whether private property is 'natural' has long been open, and considered by philosophers and anthropologists, and explored through descriptions of Utopias. He suggests that 'Other men have thought that no one form of property is natural in any sense of that word, but that all property is conventional. Then the philosophical problem is to investigate the origin and validity of the conventions upon which property rests. But whether property is thought to be natural or conventional, the question always arises as to what kind of ownership is most suited to the nature of men.' (1951:10).

What kind of property system in land and the environment is suited to our nature and to our world? This chapter explores some of the possibilities so we can see our current arrangement as just one of many current and possible forms of land tenure, of which stewardship is another. A property system, such as stewardship, that expects people to pay a market rent for the right to occupy their location of choice seems contentious only because we are immersed in a history of allocating land in quite a different way.

Classifying property systems

Each society formulates one or more property systems to describe the possessive relationship that people have with the natural world and with things. These property systems are shaped by the traditions, circumstances and beliefs of that society. In the description that follows I focus particularly on property rights that apply to land and the environment rather than to artefacts.

The conventional way of classifying property systems is according to the sort of agent that is responsible for making decisions about how the property is used. The decisions made by these agents are constrained, of course, by the legal and political frameworks of that society.

Four sorts of responsible agents have been identified since, at least, the development of Roman Law. These agents are associated with four different property systems: private property (*res privatae*), collective property (*res publicae*), common property (*res communes*) and open access regimes (*res nullius*) (Feeny et al 1990). In any society one system will generally predominate, though all may co-exist.

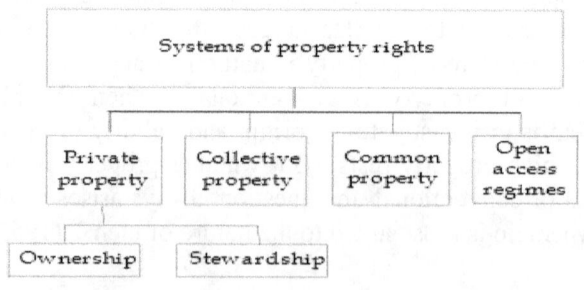

Fig 1.1 Classification of property systems

Stewardship offers an alternative to ownership of both land and the environment. In place of absolute, unconditional and perpetual ownership, it provides a use-right that is conditional on the ongoing payment of stewardship fees.

Ownership economy

Open access regimes

In an **open access regime,** anyone and everyone has the right to access and use the property. There are no restrictions or limitations on who can use it and there is no individual or body that manages the way it is used. As a consequence, there may be no cultural or economic pressures to promote its appropriate development and careful use.

Garret Hardin's provocative paper, 'The tragedy of the commons' (1968) may be understood to describe the problems of open access regimes rather than historic grazing commons:

'Picture a pasture open to all. Each herdsman tries to keep as many cattle as possible on the commons. This works well for centuries because wars, poaching and disease keep the numbers well below the carrying capacity of the land. But eventually the day of reckoning arrives. Each herdsman seeks to maximise his personal gain; he concludes that the only sensible course is for him to add another animal to his herd. And another. But this is the conclusion that is reached by each and every rational herdsman sharing a commons. Herds are increased without limit – in a world that is limited. Therein is the tragedy: Freedom in a commons brings ruin to all (Garrett Hardin 1968).

Only a small amount of land in the U.K. is now managed as an open access regime, though there are times where collective, common or private land management breaks down and a *de facto* open access regime comes into operation. The most recent claims that land is *terra nullius* were made by the imperial powers in Australia and the Americas to justify seizure of land from indigenous peoples.

Many aspects of the environment are common-pool resources, in the sense that they are diminished when they are used and difficult or costly to exclude people from using. When these are managed as open access regimes the consequences have often been dire, as, for example, in the case of the atmosphere and many fisheries. The response to these environmental problems has been to remove them from open access and apply to them some form of property rights – to transfer the open access regime into collective, private or common property.

Collective property

A system of collective property (state or public property) is one in which the use of resources is determined by reference to the intent of the collective as a whole. No one individual makes decisions about the use of collective property without reference to this intent. Collective property, in high-consumption economies (as opposed to low-consumption, 'developing' economies) is usually held by the state, by some tier of government or its arms-length agents. In low-consumption economies it may be held by the tribe.

Collective property is appropriate for some land and aspects of the environment. The hope is that the state or its agents will act as a wise and benevolent proprietor, motivated by a desire for the good of the whole and in alignment with the wishes of the electorate. In reality, the state does not have a good track record. The former state-owned industries of Eastern Europe were much more polluting than regulated private firms in the West. Governments carried on gifting electromagnetic spectrum for nearly half a century after the superior efficiency of auctions had been demonstrated (Ronald Coase (1958)). And areas of housing that have been subject to compulsory purchase orders may then be left empty and unused for long periods of time. Electoral pressure may sometimes be enough to guarantee effective management of the natural world, but at other times it clearly is not – particularly when there are powerful lobby groups promoting other interests.

Private property

A system of private property is organised around the idea that something belongs to an individual or legal entity. This 'belonging' confers on the owner the capacity to determine the use to which the property is put.

In an ownership economy both the natural world and artefacts may be held in private ownership. Even land held in trust for the public by a charitable body like the National Trust or Woodland Trust, which serves a collective purpose, is private property. The charity may provide universal access, but it can decide whether or not to do so as well as the use to which the land is put.

Private property rights been recognised since antiquity to provide incentives for the appropriate use of the natural world and artefacts. One form of incentive is economic, another is rooted in the relationship to what is possessed that private property appears to confer on the proprietor.

Common property

Common property refers to property rights that are held and managed by a defined community of commoners. It is similar to collective property in that no individual member of the community has specially privileged access, but different in that those who are not commoners are excluded, and the collective has no right to be consulted. An inshore fishery is an example of a common-pool resource, where local fishermen reach some sort of agreement about their property rights – who can fish where and when, and whether there are limits on catches.

Commoners have to negotiate how the resources will be used, and this requires the flexibility and give-and-take that is usually possible only when they know that their futures are linked or when they share a set of values. The possessions of a nuclear family, or of a religious order, are familiar examples of things held as common property in an ownership economy. Organisations like mutual societies may hold their assets as common property.

Commoners communicate and establish potentially complex rules of thumb, norms and decision-making processes for the use and extraction of resources. It is this self-organising capacity that lies at the heart of any property held in common, distinguishing it from the formal, top-down designed mechanisms deployed by the state for collective property or by individuals and corporations for private property.

The global commons

The global commons is a term that has been introduced in part to describe of resources that we all need to survive and flourish such as air, water and the cultural commons which extends beyond the arts to education and creative process. Small groups of commoners have successfully managed small scale commons, but it is not clear whether the self-organising capacities apparent at this scale can operate on a global scale. The idea of global commons is supported particularly by those who do not trust the state or its representatives to oversee the management of these resources, preferring an independent Trust with board members acting in the common good rather than a democratically elected body.

Common land

The concept of common land dates back to pre-Norman times and re-emerged after the imposition of Norman land ownership. Common land may be private or collective property, but these property rights are not absolute. Common property rights provide a means for large numbers of people to share the benefits of land that they do not own.

The first type of common land defined in the Commons Act 1965 is land over which a defined group of commoners have the legal right to carry out certain defined activities such as pasturing animals, gathering firewood, digging peat and fishing. The second type of common land defined in the Act is 'waste land of the manor not subject to rights of common', i.e., land that is unoccupied but forms part of a manor without being demesne lands (those parts of the estate reserved for the lord's use). This type of common land has no commoners, and by implication is available for use by anybody.

Some of the best-known commons, for example Wimbledon Common, used to be subject to commons rights but have been taken into collective ownership by Act of Parliament and managed for the benefit of the whole community (Marion Shoard 1987/1997: 337). This demonstrates the way in which the idea of the commons has over the course of time been separated from the management of common property rights by a defined group of commoners.

Hierarchies of property rights

Property rights may exist at a single level, for example, an individual owning outright an artefact such as a table. But property rights in the natural world are more complicated. For example, freehold property rights in land in the UK are held from the Crown and the tenants who use the land may find themselves at the tail of a series of leaseholds.

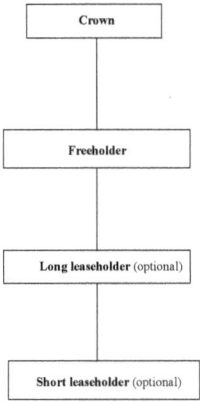

Figure 1.2

Stewardship economy

This section describes how property rights could be allocated in a stewardship economy. The steward would hold their property from a Stewardship Trust which would be autonomous and constituted within the legal system of the state. At its simplest:

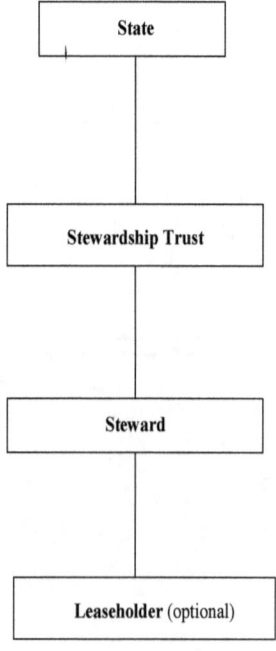

Figure 1.3

The range of possibilities for the Stewardship Trust and steward are:

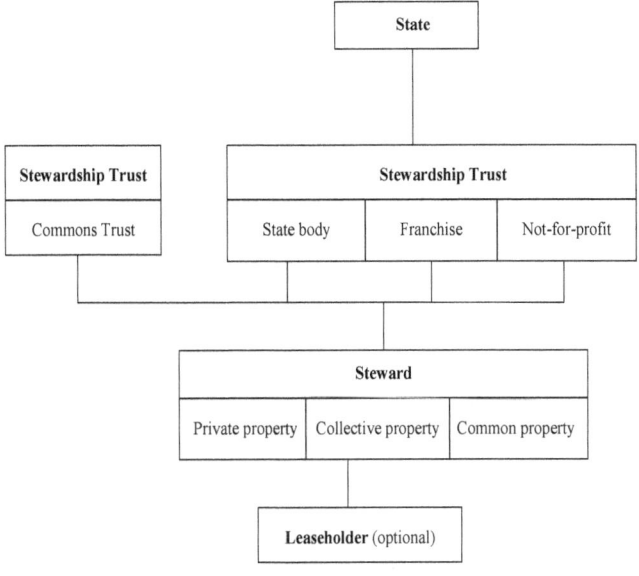

Figure 1.4

Each of these options has property rights in the form of a bundle of rights and responsibilities.

Stewardship Trust

In a stewardship economy the ultimate proprietor of land and the environment is the Stewardship Trust.

The Stewardship Trust could be formed at a variety of levels, from parish (as Thomas Spence suggested) to national level or at some level in between. The advantages of small-scale Trusts are that they can make use of local knowledge of the land and people may feel more affinity and support for local property rights of this sort. The disadvantages are the need for multiple Trust bodies and the fear that some local areas may prove to be reluctant to remit their revenue so that it can be redistributed or spent at a national level.

A Stewardship Trust may take one of several forms:

State body, which may be a government department, an arm of the state or an arms-length body, with collective property rights. This is likely to be the form favoured by socialists, who would want to retain the natural world within the realm of democratic political accountability and ensure that nobody is excluded from access to the natural world.

Franchise held from the state by a private sector enterprise and awarded by competitive tender. The ultimate property rights here remain collective, but the holder of the franchise would have short-term private property rights. This form would, like a train operating franchise or the national lottery, allow the incumbent to be displaced by a rival bidder when its franchise came to an end. This is likely to be the form favoured by libertarians, who would stress the efficiency of entrepreneurial firms and the promise that this form would maximise the proportion of the market rent that would be captured and made available as revenue.

Not-for-profit body or social enterprise with property rights that are collective or common, depending on the degree of autonomy of the trust from the state. This is likely to be the form favoured by liberals.

Commons Trust. The Trust could take the form of a self-organised Commons Trust holding property rights in common. This would be particularly appropriate for global common-pool resources for which there is no effective state or international body.

The Stewardship Trust may hold their property as private, collective or common property. While a Stewardship Trust never holds absolute private property rights it may, as a private sector body, hold a short-term franchise on these rights from the state. A Stewardship Trust may be an arm of the state, or a franchise awarded by the state, in which case the property right is collective.

On the other hand, the Stewardship Trust will hold its property in common if it is constituted independently of the state as a Commons Trust and may do so even if it is established by the state. The relationship with the regulatory or planning body is, however, different in these two cases. Commons Trusts include within themselves the role of planner or regulator and they have a fiduciary duty to preserve and manage the commons for the benefit of all. Stewardship Trusts that are subject to the state have an independent planning or regulatory body.

At the level of individual plots of land and use-rights in the environment, a stewardship economy could support private property, common property, collective property and open access regimes where these are appropriate. Stewards may be individuals, corporate bodies or other legal entities that hold private property rights or state bodies holding collective property rights from the Stewardship Trust, or groups of commoners holding common property rights.

Stewardship differs significantly from ownership in the obligations imposed on the property-holder but is nevertheless a form of private property in that it is the steward who determines how the land is used (within the usual legal and planning constraints). A steward will, for example, decide the right number of cattle – the carrying capacity of the land – and either put that number of cattle on the land themselves or arrange annual auction of grazing permits.

In a stewardship economy the state at any level of government may be a steward. That is to say, stewardship can be a form of collective property even though it is more usually a form of private property. But the state has to behave like any other steward – paying stewardship fees and abiding by the rulings of the regulator. This means that the accounts of the state body (for example, the army or local authority) make explicit the stewardship fees that they are paying. This subjects this body to a clear financial discipline and allows scrutiny of whether they are making good use of the resources.

In a stewardship economy, when several stakeholders need to negotiate the use of a common-pool resource, they would form a body (for example, a charity or social interest company) that acts as the steward of the common property regime. All stakeholders need to be included in the decision-making process of this body, as they are acting as stewards for the common property. Their property rights, like those of individuals and of the state, are conditional on paying their stewardship fees for the property.

One of the ways in which a group of commoners might decide to use their common property is to lease it to tenants and share the rent by using it for common purposes. Here the tenant has private property rights in the form of a leasehold, and the commoners have common property rights to the wealth of their common property. This parallels the situation where a national Land Stewardship Trust holds collective or common rights to the whole country, individuals have secure private leasehold rights to their plot, and everybody shares a common right to the rent paid by leaseholders.

Stewardship does not radically simplify negotiation and decision-making for common property, but it does ensure that each resource has a body that acts as its steward into the indefinite future, which makes clear costs, rights and responsibilities.

A Stewardship Trust may permit some of its property to be managed as an open access regime if there is no threat of environmental damage or overcrowding.

Chapter 2   Private property – not a single idea

This chapter presents a brief overview of several ways that private property is characterised. We are all so familiar with private property, and the particular form of private property that we call 'ownership', that we accept it as a 'given'. However, ownership is not as 'given', unchallengeable, immutable or absolute as it might seem:

❑ Private property is one of several land tenure systems that have co-existed in many different societies.

❑ With its origins in the feudal system, land in many ownership economies is held from the state and the landowner has an associated obligation to support the state.

❑ There are many different conceptions of private property of which the conventional, liberal, conception – ownership – is one.

❑ Stewardship is an alternative conception of private property.

The main focus of this chapter is the nature of the property rights that we apply to land and the environment, the natural world. When a person acquires something, whether this is natural (provided by nature) or an artefact (made by people), the common-sense view is that the term 'property' describes the possessive relationship between the person and the thing – 'it's my property'. In legal terms, however, an object cannot have a relationship as it cannot have rights and duties. 'Property', in law, refers to a relationship between the possessor and other people, enshrined as a complex bundle of rights and responsibilities referred to as 'legal title'.

Private property is distinguished from collective property, common property and open access regimes by the fact that it is an individual or constituted body that makes decisions about the use of the property.

Pre-colonial African property systems

Pre-colonial sub-Saharan Africa provides examples of private property rights to land that incorporate both use-rights for the individual and the sharing of economic benefits amongst and beyond the kinship group. However, generalisations are unreliable as systems of property rights varied over time and place, even within quite restricted areas.

The historical position has been confused by the vested interest of colonial powers in describing African land law as common property or 'communal ownership', justifying the appropriation of land from the communal ownership of the tribe to the colonial state. This provided powers (to allocate land use, amongst other things) to the hierarchy of 'native chiefs' so essential to colonial rule.

In Europe the unit responsible for defending territorial integrity and administering land law is the state. In Africa this unit was the tribe: 'It is a truism to say that West African societies were not traditionally organised within fixed territorial boundaries... Any attempt to draw up fixed boundaries and titles under these circumstances was bound to run into difficulties, and the early colonial authorities, in making such attempts, did just that' (Keith Hart 1982).

Many tribes have creation stories in which the creator of the world gives the tribe its traditional lands. The exact boundaries of such lands may not, however, have been of great importance, at least while the pressure on land was not great. Hopkins (1973) describes how extensive agriculture required not so much the ownership of a particular plot, but the right of one individual to use the property of another. Such rights might be inherited and were clearly set out, including right to the crop produced and a guarantee about tenure. The safeguards about rights to crop produced reflected the fact that it was labour which was scarce, rather than land which was generally abundant. However, Hopkins suggests that, as population grew and land use became more intensive, systems for freehold and sale of land were developed.

Jomo Kenyatta describes one system of land tenure:

'The Gikuyu defended their country collectively, and when talking to a stranger they would refer to the country, land, and everything else as 'ours', borori wittto or borori wa Gikuyu, to show the unity among the people. But the fact remained that every inch of Gikuyu territory had its owner, with the boundary properly fixed and everyone respecting his neighbour's'.

'In every district there were pasture lands where livestock grazed in common. There were also salt-licks (moonyo) and mineral springs (irori), the access to which was free to all those in the district. In addition to these there were public places (ihaaro) reserved for meetings and dances. And also, public roads and paths (njera cia agendi), as well as sacred groves... and besides this there was also woodland, reserved for building materials and firewood' (Jomo Kenyatta 1938 / 1978).

Privately owned land, commons, open access regimes and collective property are all present in this account of land tenure in Africa - as they were in Europe before the enclosures. It would be instructive to understand the ethical basis of these property rights to land. Jomo Kenyatta begins with a creation story where the founder of the tribe, Gikuyu, was given a share of land which included rivers, forests, animals.

'According to the tribal legend, we are told that in the beginning of things, when mankind started to populate the earth, the man Gikuyu, the founder of the tribe, was called by the Mogai (the Divider of the Universe), and was given as his share the land with ravines, the rivers, the forests, the game and all the gifts that the

Lord of Nature (Mogai) bestowed on mankind (Jomo Kenyatta 1938 / 1978) '.

The rest of his explanation seems to have been filtered through the ideas of John Locke (1690: V):

'In the first place the land was given to the Gikuyu by the Mogai, the Lord of Nature. Secondly, by the fact that the Gikuyu were the first to establish his homestead on the land.

Thirdly, that when the people started to multiply and to form their own family groups, each family group pegged out a portion of the forest and reserved the first rights of cultivation and hunting therein. In those days the claim of having cleared the original forest was the basic principle of absolute ownership of land. In other words, a man acquired the right to own the land through the labour he spent in developing it. For this reason, it was necessary for the whole family to join forces in order to clear sufficient land for their present and future needs. Although some form of private ownership of land existed, the system was not so obvious, as there was no property exchanged in acquiring the possession of the land.

Fourthly, when the land which the Mogai had given to the Gikuyu was thickly populated and no more forests left to be pegged out, people moved towards the forests in the south. Here the forests having been owned by the Ndorobo, there was no possibility of a man just going into the forest and establishing his claim by merely clearing the original forest. This being the case, the Gikuyu who were anxious to own the land, on seeing that the Ndorobo were willing to sell, at once started to purchase it. Thus, a new form came into being, of owning the land by purchase, instead of owning by acquiring the first rights of hunting or clearing the original forests' (Jomo Kenyatta 1938 / 1978).

This conception of private property differs from the European in the way in which kinship systems impinge on the property system. Land was the property not of an individual but of a kinship group, each living member of which had a right to the use of some of the land. The kinship group also made decisions about the use of the land taking into consideration the wishes of past generations of the group and the needs of future generations. Jomo Kenyatta stresses that property was vested in the kinship group through the owner. However, the owner did not necessarily claim exclusive use or take rent from those wanting to cultivate of build. And it is unlikely that he would sell his land without full consultation with his kinship group. This conception of private property further differs from the European in that no rent was paid for use of the land – rights to build or cultivate were granted on the basis of friendship (Kenyatta 1938 /1978).

All members of the kinship group had a claim on the land vested in the kinship group, and cultivation rights would be extended to a relative by marriage if he did not have sufficient land to maintain himself and his family.

The essential features of this property system are:

- the kinship group, which may consist of up to several hundred individuals, owns the land. Within this group use-rights for cultivation and housing are allocated according to need for land and ability to use it
- although individuals have the right to use the land, neither individuals nor the group has the right to charge rent (even to people outside the group)
- the 'owner' of the land, the *moramati*, is in fact a trustee, whose role is to husband the land for the benefit of the kinship group in keeping with the wishes of past generations and the needs of future generations of the kinship group.

Property rights in a stewardship economy probably have more in common with pre-colonial African property systems, at least amongst the Gikuyu, than with systems of land tenure that originated in Europe.

Ownership in Civil Law

The term Civil Law was taken from Roman Law, where the term was used to contrast the law of a particular state with a universal and unchanging Natural Law.

In Roman Civil Law all private property had a single owner who had outright ownership rights, affording absolutely free enjoyment and disposal of artefacts provided that this was in accordance with laws and regulations.

Roman Law was adopted in Germany in 1495, marking the time when the Roman ideas of property could be said to have taken hold in Europe (Richard Schlatter 1951: 75). Civil Law was incorporated into the Code Napoleon and spread from France, Spain and the Netherlands through their colonial empires.

Feudal system

At the time of the Norman Conquest, early Germanic law did not recognise absolute individual ownership of land. Rather, property belonged to the clan or the family, and the individual had use-rights. This theory of property underpinned feudalism, which achieved its mature classical form in England in the 11th to 13th centuries. The Domesday survey of 1086 provides a written record of the feudal order and records the wealth of the King's own demesne lands (those parts of the estate not held by tenants, reserved for the lord's use) and those of his tenants-in-chief. The guiding principle of Domesday was: 'all land held in the last resort of the king... came to us in the guise of a quiet assumption; no law forced it upon the conquered country; no law was necessary; in Normandy lands were held of the Duke, the Duke held again of the King; of course it was the same in England; no other system was conceivable' (Frederic William Maitland 1908:155).

The sovereign granted land holdings (fiefs, feuds, fees or feus) to his barons, who were required to provide military and political service according to the terms of the grant. The barons would then grant portions of their fiefs to knights who would provide service according to their grant. Nobody had absolute rights to property, everybody held their land from the sovereign. All rights to private property in land carried a responsibility to support the sovereign, whose main function was to maintain security and the rule of law. Landed property carried the duty to support this common good.

Because the feudal relationship was contractual, failure to meet its terms would constitute a breach of contract. If a vassal were found guilty of failing to perform his duties he could forfeit his fief. If the vassal felt that his lord had failed to live up to his obligations he could defy the lord and either keep the fief as his own or take it to another lord who might accept him as vassal. In either of these eventualities the matter of land ownership would probably be settled by violence.

Serfs in the feudal system were not free although, unlike slaves, the services due to their master and his power of disposal were more or less limited by law or custom. Some, such as villeins, held land from their master by customary tenure in return for agricultural work on the lord's demesne lands. The tenant's landholdings might be for his exclusive use or might take the form of common rights to grazing or cultivation.

Two factors were of particular importance in the transition away from the customary land tenure of the feudal system to ownership in common law (see below). First was the practice, adopted by lords of the manor as early as the 12th century, of commuting the forced service due on their demesne lands to a money rent, while the serfs remained unfree in the eyes of the law. By the 14th century, farm leases and money wages were increasingly taking the place of cultivation of the lord's demesne by servile labour.

Second was the increased availability of land in relation to the size of the population. The Black Death in 1348 killed more than a third of the population, and this gave power to the surviving serfs to demand greater freedoms, including freedom to own land. In the late 14th and early 15th centuries additional land became available - by assart (won for cultivation from wood or waste) as well as by leasing of demesnes.

For all these reasons, in the late 14th century customary tenure began to be replaced by either leasehold or copyhold (tenure by copy of the manorial court roll). By the mid-15th century,

Common Law in England began to protect the security of copyhold tenure. Feudal tenure persisted much longer in Scotland than in England and Wales and was finally abolished by the Abolition of Feudal Tenures etc. (Scotland) Act 2000.

Ownership in Common Law

In Common Law in England the land is the property of the state – originally the Crown ('royal estate' and hence 'real estate', as in 'real tennis'). Private ownership rights are derived from the state and are held in 'fee simple absolute', or freehold. More than one person can have rights over a particular plot of land - mineral rights, for example, may be owned by one person and surface rights by another.

Freehold includes the rights to

- o   occupy and use
- o   transfer title in whole or in part
- o   create lesser interests such as periodic tenancies, leaseholds and life interests.

These legal rights are in perpetuity but are held under the Crown, which is the ultimate owner. The Crown's position is described as 'eminent domain' – the superiority of the sovereign power over all property in the state. One manifestation of this is that if a freeholder dies without a will and with no living relations who could inherit under the rules of intestacy, the title reverts to the Crown. Another is that the state is entitled to appropriate any land required for the public good, with compensation being made to the owner. Landowners hold their land from the state, which may reasonably decide to impose obligations in return. Feudal obligations were onerous and included all the costs of providing local government, preservation of law and order, maintenance of the highways and a full share of the national defence.

Common law ownership spread through Britain's colonial empire, including the USA, Canada and India. In the USA ownership is no longer held from the state but is absolute. The power to exercise eminent domain has, however, been retained.

Leasehold

Leasehold originated in the Common Law system, though it has also been incorporated into Civil Law. Ownership of land is held by the 'ground landlord' while a 'leaseholder' or tenant is granted a 'lease' to occupy and use the land for a specified length of time. This use may be limited by internal agreements (with the ground landlord) and external constraints (for example, planning regulations). The tenant may also have security of tenure - which may be personal or transferable. If it is transferable the lease with its security of tenure may have a selling and buying price. At the end of the lease the land, along with any improvements like buildings, reverts to the ground landlord. In the UK the landlord is usually an individual or incorporated body. But the state, too, may own and lease out land and in some parts of the world – including Hong Kong, Singapore, Israel and some cities in Australia – all or most land is held by tenants from the state on long-term leases.

Liberal conception of private ownership

There are many possible detailed conceptions (specifications) of private property. The liberal conception of private ownership is embodied in both civil law and common law and comprises eleven aspects:

o   the right to possess

o   the right to use

o   the right to manage (determine how it is used by others)

o   the right to the income that can be derived (from permitting others to use it)

o   the right to its capital value (the right to receive payment at the time of sale)

o   the right to security (against expropriation)

o   the right to transfer it indefinitely by gift or bequest to another

- o the absence of any term on the possession of any of these rights
- o the prohibition of harmful use
- o the liability that certain judgements against the private owner may be executed on it
- o the expectation that, when the rights of others in the object lapse, those rights will return to him. (A M Honoré 1961:112):

The liberal conception of private property in land confers less autonomy on the owner than is often assumed by landowners in the UK. It is subject to a range of legislation and statutory rights, including:

- o eminent domain (the superiority of the sovereign power over all property in the state)
- o escheat – land reverts to the state when there are no heirs
- o the lawful rights of others – rights of way, light, support etc.
- o restrictive covenants imposed by previous owners
- o gold, silver and buried treasure belong to the Crown
- o specific legislation relating to:
    - o town and country planning
    - o public health
    - o highways
    - o housing
    - o tenancy
    - o building regulations
    - o natural resources (running water, oil, gas, coal).

What has been torn out of the heart of land ownership in the transition from feudal tenure to the liberal conception of private ownership is any sense of the duties and responsibilities that a landowner owes to other people and to the land.

We can speculate what an economy and a society would be like if one or more of the aspects of the liberal conception were changed.

24

Should the right to the income and the right to the capital value be vested in the same person? Should the term be indefinite? Should there be any limits on bequests? In a stewardship economy a steward does not have unlimited and indefinite property rights to land, but a use-right that is conditional on the responsibility to care for the land and the duty to pay a ground rent to the community.

In summary: our liberal conception of ownership is not an inevitable choice or indeed necessarily desirable. In one part of Africa, private property comes with obligations to the extended family and the wider community and proscription of the payment of rent. Even in Europe there are different conceptions of private property. In Common Law jurisdictions land is explicitly held from the state and even in Civil Law jurisdictions it falls short of an absolute property right.

The origin of private property in customary tenure and in the feudal system should remind us that it is only recently that landowners have come to expect that they can hold their land without a concomitant responsibility to support the state.

Chapter 3   Why private property?

The central debate about property rights, over the course of millennia, is whether property should be held privately or in common. Chapter 4 traces the way that thinking about common property has developed, while this chapter focuses on the arguments that have been made in favour of private ownership, particularly private ownership of land.

It is rare these days for the idea of land ownership to be a contentious issue, at least in high-consumption economies. Most people accept private ownership of land simply because 'that's the way it is' (universal consent) or 'it's recognised by the law' (positive law). If any further justification is required it is usually claimed that the original owner occupied, enclosed and improved the land and that ownership has been legitimised by the long history of exchange through voluntary contract.

Goals, Duties and Rights

Ronald Dworkin (1979/1992:171-2) proposed a classification of political theories into those that are goal-based, duty-based and rights-based. These categories are not mutually exclusive (Partha Dasgupta 2001/2004), but Jeremy Waldron demonstrates their utility by developing a valuable framework for exploring theories of property (Jeremy Waldron 1988 / 1990:64).

Goals

Goal-based theories seek to justify private ownership on the grounds that they allow some overall goal to be achieved. Such theories are pragmatic and the question is: 'what works?' Utilitarians, for example, judge social institutions by their utility;

"it is the greatest happiness of the greatest number that is the measure of right and wrong" (Jeremy Bentham 1776).

Duties

Duty-based justifications for private property assert that we have a duty to respect the property of others. They are shaped by the particular concept of duty the proponent adheres to and are often a form of revealed truth.

Rights

Rights-based theories are rooted in the idea that people have certain entitlements (rights) that may not be overridden for the sake of the general welfare. This approach has been developed to prevent the state from oppressing its citizens, or the majority oppressing a minority. A rights-based justification for private property is one that judges an individual interest in property to be sufficiently strong that it requires others (both other individuals and the state) to accept that allocation of private property.

Rights to property may take the form of **general rights** (the rights of all people to possess some property). Such rights do not provide any guidance about who should possess what, though they do explain why we accept the institution of private property. Or they may take the form of **special rights** (the right of a particular individual to possess particular property), which explain why we accept particular claims to private property.

Why we accept the institution of private property

This section explores claims that private property is justified as an institution, either because it allows society to achieve certain goals or because people have a general right to private property.

Private property may be justified on the grounds that it enables society to achieve certain goals, even if there is no exact relationship between these goals and the efforts of any individual. One set of goals is pragmatic and essentially utilitarian, that it results in the best use of land, economic efficiency, harmony, stability and security. Another set of goals are ethical, to do with self-development, fairness and liberty

Pragmatic Goals

Making good use of land

Aristotle advocated for private property partly on the grounds that it would be better cared for:

'That which is common to the greatest number has the least care bestowed upon it. Everyone thinks chiefly of his own, hardly at all of the common interest; and only when he is himself concerned as an individual. For besides other considerations, everybody is more inclined to neglect the duty which he expects another to fulfil (Aristotle Bk2:1263 Politics) (quoted Schlatter p15)'.

Private property is in general better cared-for than open access regimes, and certainly no worse than common or collective property. The reasons are complex, but it seems likely that this is largely due to a sense of personal responsibility for deciding how to use the land, combined with the security of tenure provided by private property, rather than the expectation that the owner will receive the rent and the capital gain. This is borne out by the experience of common property, which also entails responsibility and security, and may be as well cared-for as private property (Ostrom 1990).

Although the Utilitarians in 18-19th century Britain did not have a unified position on the ownership of land they held that property rights are a way of making nature more usable.

William Godwin (1756-1836) proposed a form of property in the natural world that was less absolute than the liberal conception of ownership. He described the individual as a steward on behalf of mankind who, when deciding on the way land should be used, should take into account what would produce the greatest benefit for all (not just himself).

William Godwin also advocated equality in the distribution of goods (William Godwin 1793) on the grounds that the marginal utility of goods tends to decrease with the quantity owned. When applied to land, this suggests that people should have equal access to land, or at least to the wealth of the natural world.

Economic efficiency

It has been argued that private property is economically efficient because it motivates individuals to work and provides the necessary basis for markets, which are themselves efficient. A property-rights approach may be seen to ensure sustainable management of the environment.

Hunter-gatherers need some form of (usufructuary) right to the fruits of their labour. When production is more complex and people play different roles in an enterprise, they may find it more difficult to share the product in a way that feels fair. Private property rights makes it clear who gets what reward. People are more likely to be motivated to work if we believe that we will receive the fruit of our labour, and that nobody will be free-riding on our effort. Property rights to the product of one's labour encourages work, though these may be common or collective rights.

David Hume believed that private property leads not only to increased care, but encourages useful work and production but this argument applies to artefacts rather than to the natural world:

'…. whatever is produced or improved by a man's industry ought, for ever, be secured to him in order to give encouragement to such useful habits and accomplishments'. (1748, Enquiries sect 3 pt 2: 195)

Friedrich von Hayek believed that in a market economy success and failure are unpredictable. This causes people to work, strive and innovate (Alan Ryan 1987) and, in turn, the economy functions more effectively.

Von Mises (1972:77) argued that the questions of what to produce and how to produce it are so complex that they can only be answered by a market. The market in turn requires private property.

There is widespread acceptance that we should be pursuing environmental goals. For people with 'light green' concerns the goal may be 'sustainable development' and the preservation of the earth so that future generations are not disadvantaged. People with 'dark green' concerns may not privilege humans over other species. Their goal might be the preservation and well-being of all creatures and the ecosystem as a whole. Private property rights provide a way of managing the environment sustainably by eliminating externalities.

Ethical goals

Ethical goals include: harmony, stability and security; self-development and civic virtue; fairness; liberty; duty.

Harmony, stability and security

Aristotle advocated private property, rather than collective or communal property, on the grounds that it avoids disharmony.

'When everyone has his own separate sphere of influence there will not be the same grounds for quarrel' (Politics Bk 2 1262).

The simplest way in which property reduces disharmony is by allocating goods to people and prohibiting their seizure by others. It also simplifies the distribution of the product of co-operation between a group of co-operators, each of whom may have contributed something different.

Thomas Hobbes was not unusual in believing that, in a state of nature, property was held in common but his definition of common property was novel. He imagined that 'every man has a right to every thing' – a right to every thing, not to an equal share (1642/1647 De Cive p 9-11 quoted by Schlatter 139). This is not common property as this term is usually understood, but an open access regime. In these circumstances property would be the inevitable source of conflict: 'to be every mans, that he can get; and for so long, as he can keep it.' (1651 Leviathan p 98 quoted by Schlatter 139)

In Hobbes' view property rights are a creation of the state and exist to promote the goal of stability and peace. He locates property rights in an implied social contract in which men, in order to achieve security, transfer their property rights to a sovereign who allocates and arbitrates their rights to this property.

Jeremy Bentham claimed that there are no 'natural' titles to property and that property rights may be set up in any way a legislator chooses, provided that they maximise total utility. He defended private property rights on the basis of *security*. Lack of private property rights would lead to a situation in which people feel insecure and lose the incentive to work productively and effectively. He justified the concentration of wealth in the hands of the minority, accepting that inequality was the inevitable result of security of property but that this was itself is the only guarantee of subsistence (Bentham/Bowring 1838).

Self-development and civic virtue

Aristotle (384-322BC) believed that nobody should be excluded from the class of property owners, as property allows generosity and benevolence to flourish.

'There is the greatest pleasure in doing a kindness or service to friends or guests or companions, which can only be rendered when a man has private property' (Aristotle Politics Bk 2 1134b quoted Schlatter p 17).

The belief that ownership of the land, and work on the soil, confers civic virtue on the owner has surfaced in many eras, and provide a justification for the property qualification that was required for a man to have the vote (Alan Ryan 1987:4 & Part 2).

Alan Patten (1995) points out how Hegel (1770-1831) argues that each individual needs private property if they are to develop their freedom and individuality. Their free will needs to be embodied in the external world, and appropriation of private property provides a way in which the individual endows the object with a will that is not its own. The object can only be understood by recognising the involvement of the individual's will, which displays their superiority over nature. Since the will is individual, property needs to be private.

Fairness

John Rawls (1921-2002) (1971) describes what he calls a 'well-ordered society' – one where the members are ready and able to justify to each other the way that the society is organised. In an unequal but well-ordered society the well-off are able to demonstrate to the worse-off that the society is nevertheless serving the best interests of each and every person. It is not good enough, in such a society, to make choices about the organisation of society according to their impact on the aggregate or average. A society that provides the greatest good for the greatest number is not necessarily well-ordered. Nor is a Pareto optimal society.

His argument makes use of a 'social contract' – a device for reasoning about justice, using thought experiments that describe an implied agreement about the social arrangements in a particular society. In the simplest thought experiment, where everybody has a veto in the design of the social contract, people are likely to give precedence to a variety of individual rights over societal goals.

Rawls (1971) explores 'justice as fairness' by supposing that the social contract is discussed and agreed by people over whom a 'veil of ignorance' has been drawn concerning the position and condition, and even preferences, they will have in society. Each person needs to imagine they might, for example, be fortunate or unfortunate, rich or poor, in the society they are designing. This thought experiment produces results that depend on how optimistic or risk-averse the participants are. But even risk-takers who feel comfortable with the status quo will tend to give greater consideration to the plight of the least well-off than in a social contract designed without the 'veil of ignorance'.

Thought experiments conducted behind a 'veil of ignorance' may at first seem unlikely to challenge views about private property, as people may fear that it threatens their ability to accumulate a large share of the land. But some people, particularly the risk-averse, may recognise that stewardship provides everybody with the opportunity for secure tenure of some land and support it on those grounds.

Liberty

People have long associated liberty with the right to hold private property, and particularly land.

Negative liberty is freedom from interference. Private property in land, from which you can exclude other people, is one way of reducing interference by others. This negative liberty requires the state to uphold individual rights, including the right to private property (Alan Ryan 1987: 36). Negative liberty makes private property possible.

From feudal times landed property has made it possible for an to participate freely in society - positive liberty - as citizen, soldier, politician and economic actor. But this freedom may be n no more than freedom to starve in the gutter.

Open access regimes, where strong individuals may coerce the weak, and collective property, where the state may coerce individuals, are not conducive to liberty. Private property offers a way to arrange production and distribution through the use of voluntary contracts without coercion, each person making use only of what is theirs (Alan Ryan 1987:79). Markets are less coercive than planned economies, and markets require private property.

As well as freedom from coercion, liberty needs a range of available options. Private property makes possible the expansion of options through investment and innovation.

An individual needs private property if they are to have the degree of financial autonomy that allows them to resist and protest when their liberty is infringed, particularly by the state. (Alan Ryan 1987: 88).

Goal based theories support private property rights, either as an alternative to open access regimes, common property and collective property or in addition to these forms of property rights. These property rights provide security of tenure and exclusive transferable private property rights. Goal-based theories do not suggest that

34

these rights should be free from reciprocal duties and obligations to society, and they apply equally to ownership and to stewardship.

Duty

We may accept the particular claim by an individual to a particular plot of land either because we believe that we have a duty to do so or because we recognise that they have a special right to that property. Duty-based claims to property rights have been based on either the duty to obey God or to respect the social contract.

Theology authorises private property through the duty to obey the command in Mosaic law 'thou shalt not steal'. This assumes private property and has been used to enforce existing property rights, however these may be distributed.

The ethical underpinning for feudalism, where property was held from the king, was the doctrine of the Divine Right of Kings. This provided a way to translate the duty to obey God into a duty to obey the sovereign. Every legitimate king has absolute property rights over his subjects and it was every man's duty to obey the allocation of property made by the king.

Before the Reformation, the convention was that kings ruled as the result of their appointment by God's representative on earth. After the Reformation it was held that God had given the world to Adam, who bequeathed it to a succession of kings.

Sir Robert Filmer wrote a series of political tracts between 1638 and 1652 that provided a Royalist defence for absolute monarchy. His major work, *Patriarcha* (1680) was republished in 1680 and used by the Tories to resist Whig attempts to exert some control over the monarch's actions (James Tully 1980: 53). In *Patriarcha* he attacked the idea of Natural Law, pointing out its inconsistent classifications (Robert Filmer 1680: 261 quoted James Tully 54) and dismissed Hugo Grotius' assertion that originally all things were held in common. He argued that a monarchy is a family and the king is its head; government is a patriarchy that is absolute, and the king allocated land according to his wishes.

Social contract theories are intended as devices to allow us to think about what sort of society we would choose to live in. Some writers, like Jean-Jaques Rousseau, have taken their social contract theories literally and used them to seek to justify property rights on the grounds that the individual has a duty to obey the community.

General Rights

The French National Assembly asserted in 1789, in its Declaration of the Rights of Man and the Citizen, the right to property:

'The end [in view] of all political associations, is the preservation of the natural and imprescriptable rights of man. These rights are liberty, property, security, and resistance to oppression' (Jeremy Waldron 1987).

This 'right to property' was ill-defined, though the Assembly was concerned about two pressing issues of the day, expropriation and eligibility. The Assembly wanted to ensure that the sovereign or state did not appropriate private property (expropriation). The Universal Declaration of Human Rights captures its modern form in Article 17:

'Since property is an inviolable and sacred right, no individual may be deprived of it unless some public necessity, legally certified as such, clearly requires it; and subject always to a just and previously determined compensation.' (United Nations 1948).

The United Nations General Assembly also wanted to ensure that nobody was excluded from the class of property-owners, for example on account of being a slave or a woman. Article 17 continues...

'Everyone has the right to own property alone as well as in association with others' (United Nations 1948).

The basis of this general right is that it is an essential requirement for equality. It applies not just to those with an historical claim to particular property rights, but to anybody who might want to acquire property.

Stewardship is fully compatible with the eligibility of every person to own property – indeed its claim is that everybody has the right to an equal share.

Freedom from expropriation may be raised as an objection to transition to stewardship from an ownership economy as the payment of stewardship fees leads to a fall in the price of land. The form of transition proposed in the first book of this series avoids this criticism as the stewardship fees are levied only on any increase in the price of the land over its price at the onset of transition and so does not expropriate any of the price of the land.

Both rights-based and goal-based theories provide well founded arguments for a general right to property rights. There are many possible conceptions of private property, of which the liberal conception of ownership is but one. Each of A M Honoré's bundle of rights and responsibilities could be divided amongst several different individuals, creating new conceptions of private property. New duties, rights or responsibilities could be added to or removed from the bundle (Alan Ryan 1987:54).

Special rights

Some ways of acquiring property may, from an ethical point of view, be considered so important that other people must not interfere with them. These are referred to as Special Rights (SR) to property. They are quite different from General Rights to property. Jeremy Waldron suggests that 'SR-based arguments do not... have in themselves any universal distributive implications. Those who have got hold of resources (by the specified procedures) are entitled to retain exclusive control of them; those who have not have no right to have property at all.' (1988:441). A Special Rights-based approach requires a way of describing how somebody acquires the right to own property (a principle of justice in acquisition) and a way of describing how this right may be transferred to another (a principle of justice in transfer) (Jeremy Waldron 1988).

Justice of transfer

The principle of justice in transfer has received more attention than the principle of justice in acquisition. Once title to land has been established, it is widely accepted that title may be transferred *without dilution* through contract (including sale, gift and inheritance) or by government decree (compulsory purchase). This provides the legal basis for all property transactions.

We generally accept the pragmatic position in Roman Law that property rights are held by whoever has the best title, without requiring that the title be perfect. This predisposes us not to question the fundamental rights on which this property claim rests.

Justice of acquisition

The principle of justice in acquisition is usually based either on being the creator (of an artefact) or the first occupier (of land and the environment) or on a combination of labour and occupation (the homesteader).

First occupancy

'First occupancy' is the idea that whoever first occupies a piece of land has acquired a special right to its ownership that is unconditional and perpetual.

Here I look briefly at the views of Cicero, Hugo Grotius, Samuel Pufendorf, John Locke, Immanuel Kant and Robert Nozick on the origin of property rights.

Cicero proposed that private property claims are established through long occupancy (Cicero De Officiis Book 1) and provided a useful metaphor for the preference given to those who first claim the property: 'Tho' the Theatre is common for any Body that comes, yet the place that everybody sits is properly his own'. The people who first take their seats have an exclusive right in their use, and this correlates with a negative duty on the part of others not to occupy it at the same time. But if the theatre fills to capacity, those excluded have no right to demand a seat' (James Tully 1980: 71).

Hugo Grotius was the author of Three Books on the Law of War and Peace (1625), one of the first and most influential books setting out the theory of natural rights (Richard Schlatter 1951:126). The 'natural right' he described is derived not from Natural Law but from the agreement of men (Schlatter 1951:p 131). He imagined a state of nature in which land belonged to no one and was open to all. He supposed that land, like the theatre, came to be occupied and private ownership was then adopted by universal consent based on the pattern of occupation in place at that time:

'Private ownership was introduced 'by a kind of agreement, either expressed, as by a division, or implied, as by occupation. In fact, as soon as community ownership was abandoned, and as yet no division had been made, it is to be supposed that all agreed, that whatever each one had taken possession of should be his property'' (Grotius 1625 pp 189-190).

In De Jure Naturae et Genitum (The Law of Nature and Nations, chapter 4) Samuel Pufendorf (quoted in Schlatter, 124) discussed the views of Grotius and took a less fantastical view of the origin of property rights. As people appropriated nature, argued and settled their conflicts others gave their tacit agreement.

In John Locke's Second Treatise on Government (1690/1952), he posed the question of how an individual can claim to own one part of the world, when God gave the world to all humanity in common. His answer was that individuals own the product of their labour, so land in its wild, original state would not be owned by anyone, but once an individual cultivated the land, it became his property. However, he applied a proviso, that property may be appropriated in this way only if "... there is enough, and as good, left in common for others" (Ch V. para 33).

Kant believed that the basis of property is the intent exclusively to possess something and bring it under one's will. The creator of an object owns it not because of the work expended in making it but because the act of creation is a powerful act of will. He argued there was a natural right to appropriate unowned things, including land, in a state of nature. This arose from the intent to occupy the land not the act of occupation.

Robert Nozick advances an 'entitlement' theory of property (1974:238) which treats all rights, particularly self-ownership, as property rights (Alan Ryan 1987: 2). The world is divided into things that are owned and things that are not yet owned, and when something is taken into ownership this is an unqualified freehold.

This allows him to argue that one person's special rights to property take precedence over another's general rights to, for example, life and liberty. He allowed no claim by the landless to subsistence, thought he did accept that people have a claim if they are worse off than they would have been without the institution of property (Jeremy Waldron 1988:254).

Labour

An alternative principle of justice in acquisition is that property is derived from the work carried out in creating it, an argument that works well for ownership of artefacts.

Greek and Roman philosophers had little to say about the relationship between property and work, perhaps unsurprisingly in societies in which 'slaves do all the work and masters do all the owning' (Richard Schlatter 1951:11).

In the Middle Ages there were violent disputes between church and state about the feudal property rights of kings and popes. St John of Paris provided a labour theory of private property:

'The goods of laymen... are 'acquired by individuals through their own manufacture, industry, and labour. And individuals as individuals have right, power, and true dominion' over such property and may do with it what they will so long as they injure no one else' (John of Paris 1303 Tractatus de Potestae Regna et Papali quoted Richard Schlatter 1951: 66).

In his Two Treatises on Government (Locke 1690), John Locke's purpose was to refute the absolutist claims of Robert Filmer and establish that the state has a duty to respect existing private property rights – which are not dependent on the goodwill of the sovereign or indeed on universal consent. His argument rests on Natural Law and natural rights and advances a particular special right to private property.

Robert Filmer interpreted the statement in Genesis that God gave Adam (and Eve) dominion over every living thing (Genesis I 29) as giving Adam private property and that this extended over land as well as creatures; Locke held that this right was given in common to all mankind (James Tully 1980: 60). In this situation Locke argued that an individual could claim ownership by mixing his labour with God's raw materials.

'The Labour of his Body, and the Work of his Hands, we may say, are properly his. Whatsoever then he removes out of the State that Nature hath provided, and left it in, he hath mixed his Labour with, and joyned to it something that is his own, and thereby makes it his Property' (John Locke 1690:II,27).

'He that is nourished by the Acorns he pickt up under an Oak, or the Apples he gathered from the Trees in the Wood, has certainly appropriated them to himself. No Body can deny but the nourishment is his. I ask then, When did they begin to be his? When he digested? Or when he eat? Or when he boiled? Or when he brought them home? Or when he pickt them up? And 'tis plain, if the first gathering made them not his, nothing else could. That labour put in distinction between them and common' (John Locke 1690: II,28).

Just as an apple could be acquired by the labour of picking it, a field could be acquired by tilling it:

'But the chief matter of Property being now not the Fruits of the Earth, and the Beasts that subsist on it, but the Earth it self; as that which takes in and carries with it all the rest: I think it is plain, that Property in that too is acquired as the former. As much Land as a Man Tills, Plants, Improves, Cultivates, and can use the Product of, so much is his Property. He by his Labour does, as it were, inclose it from the Common (John Locke 1690: II,32).

Special rights derived from labour allowed the English, to seek to justify private property rights in England against property claims by their sovereign. Abroad, they used it to lay claim to land wherever they could assert that indigenous peoples had not mixed their labour with the land – by which they meant enclosing it and tilling it in a European fashion.

Hegel understood property as dependent on the will of the owner, and property as acquired by marking an object as one's own. He saw this being most solid when the object has been created by the labour of the owner.

Criticisms of special rights-based theories

The special rights of first occupancy and of labour are based on the relationship between a person and a thing rather than a relationship between people. This is inappropriate on both ethical and legal grounds. The labour theory seems fair when applied to the ownership of artefacts that somebody has created, and this includes improvements to land. It is not so straightforward when the property has been produced by the labour of more than one person, by an employee, with the assistance of capital provided by another, or when production has required the use of land or natural resources.

It is easy to understand the attraction of applying the labour theory to the ownership of land and the natural world. Imagine some land that nobody currently claims to own. I decide I want to live there and build a house with my own hands. The labour theory provides a welcome justification for my ownership of the house, just as it would for the ownership of a boat that I had built. But Locke also suggests that by working on the land I have acquired the ownership not only of the house, but of the land itself. But ownership should surely be limited to the work carried out and should not include the land on which the work was done.

The theory of first occupancy leaves unclear what is meant by occupancy. Is this the first to set eyes on a plot of land, to set foot on it, to claim it for their country, or to reside there, to enclose it, improve it, employ others to improve it or use slaves to improve it? It is also unclear how extensive is the claim (the house, the farm, the county, the country, , the whole continent).

The criticism of special rights goes much deeper than the specific criticisms of the theories of first occupancy and labour. If the original acquisition of the natural world is based on any historical event, such as first occupancy or labour:

'A PJA [principle of justice in acquisition]... indicates a way in which, by performing the acquisitive act A, an individual can put not himself but everybody else under an obligation. By his act he acquires not duties but rights, and thousands of other people, including people he has never spoken with, people he has never met, people who have never even heard of him, suddenly find themselves labouring under obligations which they did not have before (Jeremy Waldron 1988:267)'.

It is all very well to imagine a golden age, a state of nature, in which some general acceptance of the principle of first occupancy did or did not arise. However, tracing ownership claims back in time leads us to quite the opposite of a golden age, to war or royal fiat (see Chapter 5).

The arbitrary nature of the theory of first occupancy is highlighted by Jean-Jacques Rousseau, whose early writings about the Golden Age included the challenge:

'The first man who, having enclosed a piece of ground, bethought himself of saying, 'This is mine', and found people simple enough to believe him, was the real founder of civil society. From how may crimes, wars and murders, from how many horrors and misfortunes might anyone have saved mankind, by pulling up the stakes, or filling in the ditch, and crying to his fellows, 'Beware of listening to this impostor; you are undone if you once forget that the fruits of the earth belong to us all, and the earth itself to nobody (1755 II 76)''.

Thomas Paine goes straight to the heart of the matter. He took the prosaic, and generous, view that the belief that it is possible to acquire land by using it was the result of a confusion that had 'stolen imperceptibly upon the world' (Thomas Paine 1797a: 6):

'There could be no such thing as landed property originally. Man did not make the earth, and, though he had a natural right to occupy it, he had no right to locate as his property in perpetuity any part of it: neither did the Creator of the earth open a land-office, from whence the first title-deeds should issue. From whence then arose the idea of landed property? I answer as before, that when cultivation began, the idea of landed property began with it; from the impossibility of separating the improvement made by cultivation from the earth itself upon which that improvement was made. The value of the improvement so far exceeded the value of the natural earth, at that time, as to absorb it; till, in the end, the common right of all became confounded into the cultivated right of the individual. But they are nevertheless distinct species of rights, and will continue to be so long as the earth endures' (1797a: 5).

Justice of transfer

Transferring property rights by voluntary contract is clearly better than taking them by force. And the principle of justice in transfer works well enough for artefacts, where labour has provided a good enough claim to their acquisition, but it is only one of many options for the transfer of private property rights in land and the environment.

It is not self-evident that acquisition, whether by first occupancy or by labour, should lead to a right to transfer property by voluntary contract. If Cicero's metaphor of the theatre is pursued, the seat would revert to the common after some period of time, perhaps, but probably after the performance and surely no later than the death of the first occupant.

Even if private property rights can be transferred from one private proprietor to another, should the rights remain undiluted? Perhaps some proportion of the property right should revert to the common each time it is transferred. Perhaps this dilution should take place not just at the time of transfer but regularly over the course of time.

Why not transfer property rights to whoever is at any time willing to carry out the most development or put it to the best use? When a private proprietor wants to stop using a plot of land, should the property be transferred to another private proprietor or should it return to the pool of common property, as is the case in some areas of sub-Saharan Africa and in Islamic law?

The principle that ownership is transferred undiluted by voluntary contract is well established in positive law but is an arbitrary choice and could be contested (Jeremy Waldron 1988:261).

When all land has been acquired, the special rights of first occupancy and labour discriminate in favour of earlier inhabitants over later inhabitants and in favour of older generations over younger generations. Newcomers are left without any access to land and the natural world, not without a seat at the theatre for one performance. Defenders of first occupancy may find this acceptable and expect that newcomers must make their fortune outside the theatre, or without access to land, and then buy their way in. But since we all need access to land to live and work this may be difficult or even impossible:

'....no Special Rights-based system of private property would be acceptable if it were not qualified by a principle of provision for basic human needs. No one can be expected voluntarily to refrain from using what is putatively the property of another if that is the only way he can see to satisfy his most pressing bodily needs. Since this is so, no-one can agree in advance in good faith to abide by a system of property which has, as one of its rules, that an owner's decision to withhold resources from the relief of desperate need must be respected. Accordingly, no system that included such a rule could possibly have been the subject of an original contract or agreement for the establishment of a just society (Jeremy Waldron 1988:439)'.

When all land is occupied, newcomers will only be fairly accommodated if there is an ongoing redistribution of land.

Pierre-Joseph Proudhon provided, in What is property? (1840), probably the most celebrated attack on the institution of private property. He made no distinction between artefacts and the natural world, though his most telling examples are all taken from the ownership of land. Having countered the justifications for property derived from positive law, universal consent and special rights originating from first occupancy and labour, he asserted that 'property is impossible' on the grounds that everybody has an equal general right to property:

'They did not forsee, those old founders of the domain of property, that the perpetual and absolute right to retain one's estate, – a right that seemed to them equitable, because it was common, – involves the right to transfer, sell, give, gain and loose it; that it tends, consequently, to nothing less than the destruction of that equality which they established it to maintain' (1840: 78 - also first occupancy 1840: 82-83 and 39-40) .

It is not necessary to agree with Proudhon's 'property is theft' (1840 xxxii), which depends on his distinction between property and possession, to conclude that Special Rights cannot provide a just or acceptable basis for claims to ownership of the natural world.

Summary: The idea of basing property rights on duty is appealing and we might accept a duty to the environment or to social justice which would specify duties to be carried out by the owner, such as those set out in stewardship's husbandry clauses.

It is difficult to imagine that we could invoke a duty to specify particular ownership claims. The special right to an artefact that somebody has created has a great deal to recommend it but is clearly inapplicable when applied to land and the environment. Special rights based in first occupancy are mistaken. The idea of basing property rights on special rights may be appealing, but we need relevant criteria that are more such as a special right that promotes environmental protection and social justice.

The focus in this chapter has been on land rather than the rest of the natural world. While stewardship of land is compelling, stewardship of the environment is surely even more so. How could first occupancy or the labour theory justify the private appropriation of oil reserves, the atmosphere or rivers? Just as with the land, use of the environment should surely require that the user compensate everybody else by the amount of its market rent – the resource rent.

Stewardship provides a new concept of private property in land. Goal-, duty- and general rights-based approaches provide a justification for stewardship that is just as satisfactory as the justification they provide for ownership and some of the relevant duties, in addition to those specified in husbandry clauses, are discussed below (Chapter 4).

Stewardship is clearly incompatible with special rights that derive from labour or first occupancy. It is, however, fully compatible with special rights that arise from an ongoing willingness of a steward to pay the market rent of their land as stewardship fees that are used for the benefit of all.

Chapter 4   Common property

This chapter explores the view that property, particularly property in the natural world, should in an ideal world be held in common (Chapter 1) rather than as private property. One of the reasons that this strand of thinking is so important is that, even though it has not led to the widespread adoption of common property, it has raised awareness that where private property rights exist they should not be absolute but should bring with them duties and responsibilities.

This chapter begins by exploring the concept of Natural Law. It then considers Judaic teachings about the Jubilee and the teachings of the Greeks, Roman Stoics, Christianity and Islam. Each of these traditions has advocated either common property or duties to others that are integral to the very idea of property. This history may seem arcane, but it has practical consequences for every aspect of contemporary economic life.

The chapter concludes by placing stewardship in the context of a tradition in which property in the natural world comes with associated duties.

Ownership economy

Natural law

Property rights are just one area in which thinkers have appealed to the idea that, by contrast with the man-made 'positive law' that is particular to each society, there exists a universal 'Natural Law' or 'Law of Nature' that governs moral behaviour and is both universal and unchanging (Cicero (54-51 BC) 3:32) (James Tully 1980: 43-50).

The relevance of any natural law relating to people and the way that they organise their lives is that, just as a sensible engineer accepts the natural law of gravity and designs drains that flow downhill, a social engineer designs interventions that are in accord with natural law.

At times Natural Law has been taken to be the rules of behaviour that would hold in an ideal world. At other times it is taken to be the rules that held in nature in some remote and idealised past. In yet other times it is taken to be the rules of behaviour intended by God. People have believed that these rules may be accessed both by reason and by revelation (which were for many centuries indistinguishable) (Richard Schlatter 1951). The challenge is how, and indeed whether, it is possible to identify any natural laws of human behaviour.

It is as well to remember that different thinkers have rather different conceptions of what Natural Law might actually prescribe and proscribe. The Stoics, for example, believed that Natural Law decreed that all things were made for the common use of man. Martin Luther believed that Natural Law was identical with the ten commandments – and that the prohibition on stealing required the existence of private property.

Many philosophers accept the three natural laws identified by St Thomas Aquinas. These are: to preserve mankind (including self-preservation); to preserve society (including promise-keeping); to worship God (Summa Theologica II. II. 94.2).

The view that land is common property in Natural Law was advanced by, amongst others, Plato, the Stoics, the Church Fathers, John Wycliffe, the Anabaptists, Franciso Suarez and Gerard Winstanley. However, the view that Natural Law also permits private property was proposed by others: Aristotle, Alexander of Hales, St Thomas Aquinas, Martin Luther, Hugo Grotius, Samuel Pufendorf and John Locke.

Judaism and the Jubilee

Leviticus makes clear that the land is the property of God, even though people may have a time-limited claim on it:

'The land shall not be sold for ever: for the land is mine: for ye are strangers and sojourners with me.' (Leviticus 25 xxiii).

Private property in land would be subject to regular and predictable land reform:

'And ye shall hallow the fiftieth year, and proclaim liberty throughout all the land unto all the inhabitants thereof: it shall be a jubilee unto you; and ye shall return every man unto his possession, and ye shall return every man unto his family (Leviticus 25 x).

'And in all the land of your possession ye shall grant a redemption for the land' (Leviticus 25 xxiv).

'...that which is sold shall remain in the hand of him that hath bought it until the year of jubilee: and in the jubilee it shall go out, and he shall return unto his possession'(Leviticus 25 xxviii).

People may have property rights in the things that they make, including most buildings, although some buildings are understood to revert to nature:

'And if a man sell a dwelling house in a walled city....(it) shall be established for ever to him that bought it throughout his generations: it shall not go out in the jubilee. But the houses of the villages which have no wall round about them shall be counted as the fields of the country' (Leviticus 25 xxix-xxxi).

The rabbinical view is that the Jubilee was instated primarily to ensure that the original allotment of the Holy Land among the tribes was maintained. It is sometimes interpreted as an ideal rather than a practical reform. The proposal for the Jubilee underlies the 49-year leaseholds that apply, in theory, to much of the land of Israel. It suggests a very clear statement of underlying morality – that the land belongs to God, all people must be able to access and to benefit from the land, and the security of tenure necessary for daily life and for the improvement of land is limited (to fifty years).

According to Leviticus, private property in land is not absolute. It is limited in time, and ownership is limited by the requirement to return it to its original owner at the Jubilee.

Greece

Plato described two different property systems, each presented as an ideal (Richard Schlatter 1951: 11). In the *Republic*, which has been widely interpreted as a political treatise as much as an allegory, he described the ideal society as 'a city which would be established in accordance with nature' (Plato: Republic 428-9). In this ideal society those who produce the wealth own property but have no political power. The Guardians, who exercise political power, have no personal property but hold property in common (Plato: Republic V).

In his more practical *Laws* (360BC/2016) he recognised that the ideal of an uncorrupted political elite was not achievable and proposed allowing citizens to hold both political power and private property. Every man held a minimum amount of land, and nobody could hold more than four times that amount.

Aristotle proposed that in an ideal state (Politics Bk VII), half the land should be privately owned by citizens (Chapter 3). The other half was to be held by the citizens in common and worked by publicly-owned slaves (Richard Schlatter 1951: 13). He stressed the importance, in the realm of private property, of equality of property – particularly of land (Richard Schlatter 1951: 18).

The Greeks shared the view that common property was an ideal, but private property a practical necessity. They variously advocated leaving some land in common and restrictions on private property that limited holdings to an equal share.

Rome

Cicero, as noted above (Chapter 3), defended private property in a society that was even more unequal than Greece. He justified this by distinguishing between Natural Law (ius naturale) that was universal and unchanging, under which property is held in common and Civil Law (ius civile) that was peculiar to a particular state, under which property was private.

In spite of drawing on the teaching of Cicero, the Roman jurists failed to make clear whether they viewed property as natural or conventional. This meant that later writers were able to find support for either view when they argued for either common or private property rights (Richard Schlatter 1951: 30).

In practice the Roman republic enacted a series of Agrarian Laws, each limiting the amount of land that any one person could hold.

Stoics

The Stoic school of philosophy was initiated in Greece by Zeno of Citium (337-262 BCE). It spread to Rome where one of its most renowned advocates was Seneca. The Stoics' great difference from Plato and Aristotle was that they believed that all men were equal before the law, and that neither class nor slavery could be justified (Richard Schlatter 1951:23). They believed that there is a purposeful order to the universe, and the way to live in accordance with this order is to obey Natural Law, according to which all things were made for the common use of men. But they accepted that, as human nature is corrupt, private property was necessary in the world as it is.

Seneca (5B.C – 65A.D), a Stoic philosopher, described in his letters a primitive age when men 'enjoyed nature and shared her amongst them…' But into this ideal arrangement came avarice: 'craving to sequestrate and appropriate something to itself, it succeeded only in making everything somebody else's and reduced itself from the immeasurable to the inconsiderable'. 'Avarice dissolved the partnership and impoverished even those whom it made richest, for in their desire for personal possessions they forfeited universal possession'.

Seneca quotes the passage from the first book of Virgil's Georgics describing a time when

'No fences parted fields, nor marks nor bounds

Distinguish'd acres of litigious grounds;

But all was common…' (Dryden 1697)

Here in Seneca is the full theory of a state of nature where property was common and used equally by all for the satisfaction of needs. This suggested that private property was not natural was justified only because human nature was corrupt, making such arrangements necessary to preserve even a modest amount of law and order. This theory was, in an ambiguous form, incorporated into Roman Law and thence by Christian writers. (Richard Schlatter 1951:25-26).

Christianity

This section draws heavily on the writings of Richard Schlatter (1951).

Several of the parables of Jesus refer to the stewardship of possessions, and this metaphor carries the suggestion that Christians should regard the whole of creation as the property of God. Jesus taught his followers to give away their property to the poor and warned of the pitfalls of wealth. The early Christians 'had all things common' (Acts of the Apostles 4:32 NIV) and Acts 2:44, 'All believers were together and had everything in common' and Acts 2:45, 'They sold property and possessions to give to anyone who had need'. Jesus provided no support for the institution of private property.

The early Church managed to reconcile Christ's teachings about the pitfalls of wealth with the existing private social order, including property rights, by drawing on the distinction in Roman Law between Natural Law (ius naturale) and Civil Law (ius civile or ius gentium). The Golden Age described by the Greek philosophers, when men lived according to Natural Law and property was common, was equated with the garden of Eden in which 'God gave dominion...' (Genesis 1:28). The idea that in Natural Law all property is common found its way in to the canon law of the mediaeval church. The need for conventional Civil Law was explained by the fallen nature of man (Richard Schlatter 1951:35) from the stories of the Garden of Eden and the Fall of Man.

Christian debates about property over the next two millennia have been dominated by the doctrine of the Fall and by different interpretations of the nature of the dominion granted by God in Genesis. A minority view, held by the Anabaptists from 16th century and the Diggers (17th century) amongst others, held that God had given dominion to mankind in common, and that even fallen man should hold property in common. The majority view has been that God gave dominion to Adam and his heirs, and that fallen man should hold private property. However, since God had created all things common, Christians had a duty of charity and private property should be distributed fairly. The debate was active amongst the church fathers with St Cyprian, St Chrysostom and St Ambrose all advocating sharing of property or common property while St Augustine advocated private property (Richard Schlatter 1951:39).

St Ambrose *(c337-397)* held that only God, as creator, could have dominion over the Earth. Since men could not have dominion over the earth, private property is not natural and all things are made for the common use of men *(*Richard Schlatter 1951:36*)*.

St Augustine *(354-430)* argued that while divine law applied to the state of nature, human law had been introduced and remained necessary because of the corruption of human nature brought about by the Fall. Divine law advocated common property (which was possible, and desirable, in an ascetic monastic life) but sinful men would be unable to cope with common property, 'human nature being what it is', so private property was appropriate (Richard Schlatter 1951: 37-40). So, the ideal of common property is upheld and private property justified by the doctrine of original sin.

By the Middle Ages the Church was richer and more powerful than most temporal powers, but this sat uncomfortably with the medieval view that private property was the consequence of sin.

Scholastic philosophy arose from Christian monasteries and dominated medieval universities from around 1100 to 1700. The early scholastic philosopher, **Alexander of Hales** (c1185-1245) proposed that the law of nature prescribes common property for men without sin but that it also prescribes private property for men as they are now, after the Fall (Richard Schlatter 1951:44). Private property is still the result of sin, but now sanctioned by Natural Law and not merely conventional.

St Thomas Aquinas (1225-1274) makes no mention of private property being required by man's sinful nature, or of common property in a state of innocence, though he does hold that common property or no property at all is the most perfect form of property (Richard Schlatter 1951:50-54). He went further than Alexander of Hales and argued that private property (for example, clothing) was an addition to the state of nature rather than an alternative, and therefore natural and good. In his reply to Ambrose, he agrees that dominium over things is natural to God alone but asserts that dominium over the use of things is natural to man. (Summa Theologica (written 1265-1274) II 66 1). In the economy of his time this category of use-rights consists largely of agricultural produce – artefacts. Here then is a distinction between the natural world, which is God's, and artefacts, for which ownership is appropriate.

By the time of the Reformation, the doctrine of the Fall had neutralised Christ's teachings for most Christians and permitted the Roman Catholic Church to amass both wealth and temporal power. Radical Christians were inspired to create anew the perfect world of the Garden of Eden, for example in monastic life.

In the 14th century **John Wycliffe** (c1328-1384, translator of the Bible and Roman Catholic dissident) and his followers, the Lollards, advocated communal property and strove to imitate the poverty of Christ and his disciples.

In the 16th century the **Anabaptists** advocated the establishment of egalitarian Christian communities in which goods were held in common. While **Martin Luther** (1483-1546) acknowledged that 'in Christ's community' everything is in common (Richard Schlatter 1951: 78), he was deeply opposed to the Anabaptists and attacked their proposals for common property. Luther believed that Natural Law was identical with the Ten Commandments. Private ownership has as its foundation 'Thou shalt not steal'. So, it is God's command that is the formal basis private ownership and the authority of princes, and this avoids radical proposals to interfere with those rights and that authority on the grounds of utility and the common good. As man's reason is debased, Luther considered that that they should not appeal to natural laws and rights' (Richard Schlatter 1951: 90-92). This removed property from the realm of rights and located it as a duty to respect the status quo.

John Calvin (1509-1564), in his *Institutes of Christian Religion*, placed his faith primarily in the Bible and therefore in the right to private property enshrined in the Ten Commandments. He accepted, though, that in temporal matters it may be possible to identify by reason some universal principles or natural laws. Calvin developed the medieval idea that men held their lands as vassals of God into one in which they were stewards. The right to use land brought with it moral responsibilities and obligations and required the owner to put the property to good use (Richard Schlatter, 1951:101).

Robert Crowley (1517-1588), a Tudor Protestant clergyman, printer and polemicist) accepted that property was authorised by God to prevent the strong oppressing the weak but argued that the earth belongs to all men and that individuals can claim only what they have gained by the sweat of their faces. Great wealth is not held by natural title but is given to men by God and they are to use it as his stewards.

Natural rights (and connection with Natural Law)

Natural rights are sometimes traced back to the struggles of nobles for rights against the king in 1215 (Magna Carta) and of the people for rights against their feudal lords in 1217 (Charter of the Forest). But natural rights had emerged within the doctrine of Natural Law in 12th century Bologna before being developed by **William of Ockham** (c1285-1347) and achieving widespread recognition during the Enlightenment. St Thomas Aquinas had not used the language of rights but the revival of his thought in the 16th century (neo-Thomism) grounded the concept of rights in his conception of Natural Law. This provided the major ideology of the Catholic counter-reformation, which brought about a major shift from qualified to absolute private property rights.

The rules of behaviour prescribed by Natural Law are shaped by the sort of the 'state of nature' that its advocates believed had preceded the appearance of private property. Some, like Francisco Suarez, have imagined a state of common property from which all of humankind derived an *inclusive* general right *to* their share of the whole. Others, like Hugo Grotius and Samuel Pufendorf, have imagined an open access regime, from which individuals have carved out *exclusive* private property rights *in* some part of the world.

The Jesuit theologian **Francisco Suarez** (1548-1617) (The laws and God the lawgiver 1612) distinguished between *ius in re* (a right in a thing) and *ius ad rem* (right to a thing). The former is an exclusive right, which prevails against the world, to something that is already possessed, including the right to exclude others from it. The latter is an inclusive right to be included amongst those who have a claim without, as yet, possessing.

Suarez follows Aquinas in stating that, according to Natural Law, there is common ownership of the natural world, but he clarifies that this common right is an *ius ad rem*, a right to share in not a right to exclude. (Tully p68) If all men have an inclusive common right to land, the question remains how this property right is to be individuated. Suarez doesn't see this as a problem and assumes that man will divide the earth and share it as needed. (Tully p60) From this perspective, private property in land is qualified by the right of others to an equal share.

The lawyer **Hugo Grotius** (1583-1645) was employed by the Dutch East India Company to justify their policy of piracy. He did so by challenging the Portuguese claim to a monopoly of trade to India, which he treated as a form of property right. He claimed that property presupposes occupation, and that the seas had never been occupied – that they are open access regimes. Land, by contrast, had passed from belonging to nobody as people had appropriated what they needed (for the purpose of self-preservation) and, if they could get agreement, laid claim to land (Schlatter p 139). Whatever a person first lays hands on becomes their private property, and on the same grounds they have the right to defend it by force. (Tully p80 – see Grotius Book II Ch 2)

Grotius held that the term 'dominium', the right to common property (*ius ad rem*), had come to mean 'property in' (*ius in rem*) – and so that the terms dominion (*dominium*) and private property (*proprietas*) had come to mean the same thing. [c.f. pp Tully 71] In this way he denies that common property refers to an inclusive *ius ad rem* and asserts that it refers to an exclusive *ius in rem*, the right to a *share* of the earth. Once this share is established, it is unqualified. In this view the earth has been transferred to private property not from common property but from an open access regime. Private property arises when it is occupied and there could not have been a time at which the Earth was the common property of mankind, because this would have predated its occupation (James Tully 1980: 69). This marked the beginning of claims to unqualified private ownership, uncluttered by prior claims of common 'rights to'.

The Lutheran **Samuel Pufendorf** (1632-1692) accepted Hugo Grotius' definition of property and extended his argument. Unlike Grotius, who held that in a state of nature there are joint rights, Pufendorf argued that a state of nature amounted to a state of 'negative community' in which 'common ownership' meant that nothing belongs to anyone, and everything is in a state of no-ownership (Richard Schlatter 1951: 145 referring to Pufendorf Bk 4 Ch 4).

'The word 'communion' is taken either *negatively* or *positively*. Things are said to be common in the former manner insofar as they are considered previous to any human deed which declares them to belong more especially to this person than to that. They are also, in the same sense, said to be *no one's*, that is, in the negative sense of not yet having been assigned to anyone in particular rather than the private sense of being incapable of such assignation. And they are referred to as common stock available to all. Things common in the other sense, however, differ from those that are one's own in this point only, that they belong to several persons in the same manner while the latter belong only to one.

Now ownership or dominion is the right by which a thing's substance, as it were, belongs to someone in such a way that it does not belong wholly to another man in the same manner. For dominion and ownership are to us one and the same.....' (from Book 4 CH 4 sect 2 of Pufendorf – modern translation quoted Vallentyne & Steiner 2000)

'God Himself by no means prescribed some universal manner of possessing things that all men were bound to observe. And so things were made neither proper nor common (in a positive communion) by an express mandate of God, but were constituted as much by men later on as the tranquillity of human society required....' .... Therefore, the ownership of things flows directly from a tacit or express agreement among men. (from BooK 4 CH 4 sect 4 of Pufendorf – modern translation quoted Vallentyne & Steiner 2000)

'It is plain that before all human agreements there was a communion of all things. Not a positive communion, of course but a negative one.' (from Book 4 CH 4 sect 5 of Pufendorf – modern translation quoted Vallentyne & Steiner 2000)

There are no inclusive common property rights (ius ad rem), so there is no need for agreement to dispense with them. All that is needed is a pact, which may be implicit, to respect the occupier as the proprietor who holds an exclusive private property right (ius in rem). Samuel Pufendorf also argues that property is a right in the substance of a thing. This runs counter to the Thomist (and Lockean) view that the substance of the earth belongs to God and man's dominion is limited to the use of the natural world.

Suarez believed that common ownership of the natural world should prevent anybody from being excluded from private property. Hugo Grotius argued that the Earth could not have been common property and there was no impediment to claims to private property. Samuel Pufendorf extended this argument to claim that people only required a pact to bring in to being exclusive private property – and that this property was a right to the substance of a thing not just to a use-right. Here was a justification for private property that is unqualified by any duties and applies to the natural world as well as artefacts.

The 16th and early 17th centuries saw a rapid increase in the population of England without significant increase in food production. Poverty and hunger were aggravated by enclosure of common land and by farm consolidation. In the aftermath of the English Civil War and the regicide of January 1649 there was naturally a debate about how to allocate the lands confiscated from the Crown and the church (Christopher Hill 1973:20).

John Lilburn and the Levellers advocated parcelling out the confiscated lands of the Crown and the church in order to broaden the social base of private ownership. They repudiated **Jerrard Winstanley** (1609-1676) who experienced a revelation that 'the earth shall be made a common Treasury of livelihood to whole mankind, without respect of persons' (Jerrard Winstanley 1649 a). Referring to himself a 'True Leveller', he called for the abolition of private property and on the 1st April 1649 led a band of about 40 **Diggers** and began to dig uncultivated common land on George Hill in Cobham, Surrey:

'for I took my spade and went and broke ground upon George-hill in Surrey, thereby declaring freedome to the Creation, and that the earth must be set free from intanglements of Lords and Landlords, and that it shall become a common Treasury to all, as it was first made and given to the sonnes of men' (Jerrard Winstanley 1649 a).

The Digger movement was by no means the first or the last encroachment on the land, and the Cobham colony of 11 acres lasted little more than a year but Winstanley's eloquence and passion provided it with the force to become a national movement, albeit briefly, and a lasting source of inspiration.

'Was the earth made to preserve a few covetous, proud men to live at ease, and for them to bag and barn up the treasures of the Earth from others, that these may beg and starve in a fruitful land, or was it made to preserve all her children?' (Jerrard Winstanley 1649 a)

Jerrard Winstanley was advocating common property. It extended to artefacts, though his focus was on the land.

Like Suarez and unlike Grotius and Pufendorf, John Locke (1632 - 1704) believed that God had given the earth to mankind as a whole, in common, and set out: 'to shew, how Men might come to have a property in several parts of that which God gave to Mankind in common.' This led him to qualify his defence of private property rights in two ways. The first of these was that nobody should bring into their possession goods that will perish uselessly – intended no doubt to apply to natural produce like fruits but able to be interpreted as a prohibition against owning land that is left idle. The second, and most significant, was the so-called 'Lockean proviso'.

Although John Locke believed that it is possible to acquire special rights to property through labour or first occupancy, this applied only where it did not exclude others from land:

'Nor was this appropriation of any parcel of Land, by improving it, any prejudice to any other Man, *since there was still enough, and as good left*; and more than the yet unprovided could use. So that in effect, there was never the less left for others because of his enclosure for himself (John Locke 1690: II,33 – my italics.

He believed that every citizen has a fundamental general right, derived from the first Natural Law that mankind ought to be preserved. This right to subsistence, to preservation, could be discharged if they had:

• as much land as they can make use of – or
• 'enough, and as good' land, if land is in short supply – or
• the general benefits of living in a society characterised by money, rent and unequal land ownership – on the condition that this provides greater benefit than living in a society in which each has a share of the land – or
• access, at the very least, to subsistence (a 'living')

(John Locke 1690).

Although this is widely interpreted to amount to the advocacy of a general (inclusive) right to property, Jeremy Waldron (1988:218) does not think it goes as far as this.

The Lockean proviso allows this right to a 'living' to be divorced from the property system and provided, for example, by a tax-benefit system.

Locke's concern was land, not artefacts. He believed that those who owned land had a duty to leave an equal share of land for those who do not have any. He diluted this requirement, and divorced it from land ownership, by accepting as an alternative the provision of 'a living'.

This right to subsistence has been denied by a line of thinkers, including **Thomas Malthus** (1766–1834), who declared that human beings for whom nature refuses to provide were constantly brought into the world and that they:

'have not the slightest right to any share in the existing store of the necessaries of life' (1798).

In the Roman Catholic Church **Pope Leo XIII** (1810-1903) endorsed the labour theory of special rights in his encyclical 'Rerum Novarum' (1891) and **Pius XI** (1857-1939) removed all reference to natural rights (Richard Schlatter 1951: 279.

In his book, 'A Theology of the Built Environment: Justice, Empowerment, Redemption', the theologian, Tim Gorringe concludes that possession can never be absolute, and that Christianity requires stewardship on behalf of all (2002:77).

Islam

Islam teaches that private property in land should be put to use. The ruler or state donates land to those who need it and are able to use it. Unused land reverts to the state, thereby refreshing the pool of land available for donation. This provides an example of a successful qualification of the individual need for security of tenure by the need of all for access to the land. The system is, however, placed under increasing strain when the pool of available land disappears.

A system of ownership leaves unresolved the gulf between the desirable, Natural Law, and the actual. The result is a polarisation between the view that property should be held in common and the view that it should be held privately. Although the system of private property currently prevails, there is a widespread belief that there are many things that should be held in common or collectively. People recognise that private property must come with certain qualifications and responsibilities toward those who are excluded from a fair share of land and that they need to be provided with an income in compensation for that exclusion. But from the perspective of poor people in a high-consumption economy, spending by the rich is as wasteful as leaving fruit on the trees and forbidding the hungry to pick it. From the perspective of people in low-consumption economies the behaviour of people in high-consumption economies could be seen as even more outrageous.

Is the choice between private property and common or collective property an either/or choice? Or is there some way in which we could have the best of both worlds – common property for resources over the long term, for example, combined with private property for use-rights?

Stewardship economy

How does common property fare in a stewardship economy?

Artefacts and the natural world

Stewardship economy: private property without private ownership makes a clear distinction between artefacts and the natural world. Private property rights in artefacts are absolute, not qualified. But private property rights in the natural world are qualified by the duty to compensate others by paying the market rent into a fund to be used for the benefit of all.

Natural Law

By distinguishing between artefacts and the natural world and ensuring that the market rent of the natural world is made available for the common benefit of all, stewardship provides both common property rights held by the Stewardship Trusts and private property rights held by private proprietors.

In this way stewardship is fully supportive of the first Natural Law – the preservation of humankind. And Natural Law as interpreted more broadly provides at least as much justification of stewardship as of any other form of property rights.

Stewardship is a system of exclusive private *property rights in* the earth, as it is individual stewards who occupy and decide what use to make of their sites.

The Land Stewardship Trust and the Environment Stewardship Trusts hold the whole of the natural world in trust, providing inclusive common or collective *property rights to* the market rent of the natural world. Stewardship answers the question of how the common property should be used: it should be used by those stewards who are prepared to compensate others by meeting the general right to all for subsistence. In this way, stewardship reconciles the benefits of private ownership (including security of individual tenure and the freedom to buy, sell and trade artefacts) with the ethos of sharing and equality of opportunity provided by the common treasury of market rent.

Stewardship ensures that the benefit derived from any piece of land (its rent) is not monopolised by one individual or family. While the Jubilee operates intermittently every 50 years to redistribute land, stewardship continuously shares the market rent of land so that everybody benefits all the time and can use their share to access land.

To summarise

Owners claim the right to exclude others from their private property. However, for millennia there has been the view that land should ideally be held in common and that owners have a duty to support the basic institutions of society and to ensure the survival and subsistence of those they exclude from their land. A different view, that private property rights are unencumbered by any counterbalancing duty, originated in Hugo Grotius' defence of piracy and was explicitly taken up by Thomas Malthus and Robert Nozick. This view, in which the natural world is seen in the same way as artefacts, has become the unthinkingly accepted norm. Even so, societies based on this view have fallen short of accepting Malthus' and Nozick's belief that those without private property have no right to subsistence or indeed survival and have assembled the apparatus of the welfare state to provide this means of subsistence. But, in doing so, they have divorced this duty from the holding of private property in the natural world.

Stewardship explicitly re-unites the private property-holder's right to occupy and exclude with their duty to support society and others. By making property in land and the environment conditional on the payment of stewardship fees it ensures that property rights in artefacts are completely unqualified – even by taxation. It removes the need for the taxes and benefits that otherwise have had to be devised to deal with the consequences of unqualified private ownership. And it puts common ownership of the wealth of the natural world at the heart of property relations.

Chapter 5   Coercion and its legacy

The single most important justification provided for private property in the natural world is the special right of first occupancy – that an original owner acquired rightful private property rights by being the first occupier of previously unoccupied land.

Most current owners of land have acquired it by entirely legal, consensual and non-violent means   But when the chain of transfers is traced back in time it is impossible to find a link back to a true first occupier.   Most land titles for which there is a complete historical record can, by contrast, be traced back to a time when it was acquired by conquest, force, or trickery and very often there have been subsequent legal dispossessions as the result of royal fiat or statute.

Few titles in England, for example, can be traced back before the conquest of 1066.   Title to land in the eastern states of North America can, at least in principle, be traced back to acquisition from Native Americans either by force or by a process of 'purchase' that clearly meant something quite different to the two parties.   In South America acquisition was by conquest and regulated by the decision of the Pope to divide undiscovered lands, populated by non-Christians, between the kings of Spain and Portugal.

The purpose of this chapter is to provide a few examples to remind the reader of this history of violence and deception that underlies the reality of current ownership claims.   It illustrates the shoddy ethical basis that underlies all ownership economies.

'Get off this estate'
'What for?'
'Because it's mine'
'Where did you get it?'
'From my father'
'Where did he get it'
'From his father'
'And where did he get it?'
'He fought for it'
'Well, I'll fight you for it'

(Carl Sandburg 1936)

'Violence, fraud, the prerogative of force, the claims of superior cunning – these are the sources to which those titles may be traced. The original deeds were written with the sword, rather than the pen: not lawyers, but soldiers, were the conveyancers: blows were the current coin given in payment; and for seals, blood was used in preference to wax' (Herbert Spencer 1851: sect 3 of Ch 8-10)

Marx' Capital I: 'Of the so-called primitive accumulation' (Pt 8 pp 873ff Penguin) – capitalist exploitation originated in the forcible expropriation of small farmers thrown off the land and offered the non-choice of working as labourers or starving.'

United Kingdom

In *Who owns Britain: the hidden facts behind landownership in the UK and Ireland*, Kevin Cahill (Kevin Cahill 2001/2: 20) describes three great 'land grabs' that have, along with the more insidious enclosure movement, defined landowning in the UK over the last millennium – the Norman Conquest, the Reformation and the Commonwealth.

Norman conquest

The Anglo-Saxons had a well-developed land ownership system but, on his accession after the Battle of Hastings, William claimed the right to all the land in England. He confiscated the land of the English lords who had fought with Harold at Hastings and distributed it to the 1400 tenants-in-chief that he appointed from among his Norman supporters.

Kevin Cahill describes how John Bateman (1876) used the 1872 *The Return of Owners of Land* to identify 1500 landowners in England and Wales with more than 3000 acres (Kevin Cahill 2001/2: 42). The concentration of land ownership inaugurated at the Conquest has persisted, remarkably unchanged, for at least 800 years. Title to land in England can, in principle, be traced, through a series of purchases and bequests, to the military conquest of 1066 - not to some social compact, agreement, labour or first occupancy but to violence, bloodshed and dispossession.

Reformation

The next historical moment at which a wholesale transfer of land ownership took place was the reformation. The dissolution of the monasteries by Henry VIII served both to break the power of the Catholic church in England and to provide the king with 10 million acres, much of which he distributed to supporters willing to impose the new Church on their local areas.

Civil war and Commonwealth

The Commonwealth, formed in 1648, abolished the monarchy and the House of Lords. To meet its expenses, it sold land from the Church Estate, Crown Estate and the Royalist estates that it had acquired (probably millions of acres). The Restoration in 1660 returned many of the English, but not Irish, Royalist estates to their former owners.

Enclosures

In Europe in the Middle Ages, private land ownership was widely qualified by the 'rights in common' that commoners held to use the land, often for specific purposes such as grazing or ploughing.

The enclosure of land to which others held rights in common began in England in the 12th century. It was causing sufficient distress to peasants and tenant farmers by the mid-thirteenth century that statutes in 1235 & 1285 provided for enough unenclosed land be left to fulfil the ploughing and common grazing rights of tenants.

Enclosures continued over the centuries, gathered pace in the mid-18th century and continued till the mid-19th century. Consolidation of land holdings contributed to improved efficiency of land use, but the landless and customary tenants were excluded from the land. The process was legal, in the sense that it was made possible by Acts of Parliament. But, given the property qualifications required for standing as a Member of Parliament, or even voting, and the extensive landholdings of members of the House of Lords, the enclosures were clearly coercive.

The enclosures were not a matter of nibbling away at the edge of the village green. Over 7.5 million acres of common land were enclosed under Acts passed between 1710 and 1843. (Henry George 1879 Book VII Chapter IV:340). The Duke of Sutherland enclosed more than 1.25 million acres, the Duke of Buccleugh close to 0.5 million. (John Chapman 1987)

Clearances

Highland clearances

After the Jacobite uprising in 1745 the English sought to destroy the clan system and its feudal land tenure in the Highlands. The right of a clan chief to demand military service from their tacksmen was replaced by the demand for payment of rent, and lands were enclosed. At the same time, agricultural developments led to a shift from subsistence farming to large-scale cattle and sheep farming. This combination of factors led to a rapid and often brutal depopulation during the first half of the 19th century. It is estimated that about 150,000 Highlanders and Islanders were cleared from their ancestral lands over the course of a century, about half the total population of the area in 1800.

Great Irish famine

The great Irish famine followed the failures of the potato crop in the 1840s, at which time Ireland was part of the United Kingdom of Great Britain and Ireland. A quarter of the population sought Poor Law relief, and probably more than a million people died between 1846 and 1849 from under-nutrition and infectious disease. In 1847 the infamous 'Gregory clause' introduced into the Poor Law legislation excluded from relief any family holding more than a quarter of an acre unless they gave up their land. This led, unsurprisingly, to widespread clearances, and landowners turned to rearing livestock. Perhaps as many as half a million people were evicted and between one and two million people emigrated between 1845 and 1855, numbers at the time unprecedented in the history of international migration (Colm Toíbín 1998:17).

Indigenous peoples and their land

Indigenous peoples generally have an understanding of ownership of land and the natural world that differs from that found in ownership economies. Most place greater emphasis on communal access and common rights to land, and less on individual rights and ownership. Indeed, the approach of indigenous peoples seems closer in spirit to stewardship than to ownership. Colonial and post-colonial powers have expropriated traditional lands for mining, logging, settling or in the name of 'development'; and it is still the profits from owning the natural world and extracting resource rents that drives encroachment on the lands of indigenous peoples.

North America

Between the 17th and 19th centuries Europeans took possession of almost the whole of the USA from the Native Americans. A series of treaties were signed following decisive military conquest, describing the transfer of land as mutually agreed market transactions.

Sale of land held a meaning for the Native Americans different from that for the colonialists. The indigenous peoples had a range of well-developed systems of land tenure, but these did not include buying and selling land amongst themselves. The idea of a fenced-off piece of land was not a useful concept for people who made use of the land by moving their villages in response to the changing environment. Land transactions with the colonialists took place within a legal system that was foreign to them.

These factors suggest that, although 'purchases' were made, there was a large element of coercion in the transfer of land from the indigenous peoples. Indeed, after the War of Independence the new American government insisted that Native Americans, most of whom had sided with the English, had forfeited all claims to their land and that this could be appropriated without compensation (Eric Foner 2006:17).

Powerful individuals and firms bought or were granted great tracts of land that established their power base and provided the foundations for wealthy dynasties. One of the most significant interventions was the Dawes Severalty Act of 1887 which broke up the system of common property, according to which the tribe held land in its entirety in common, and replaced it with a system of private property in which land was held in severalty by individuals. The individually owned plots that this permitted could then be re-allocated and sold, and the result of this process was that Native Americans lost 86 million acres of land. This abuse was widely justified by the claim that indigenous peoples were 'primitive' or 'backward'.

One of the central issues is whether collective or common title to land, rather than individual title, is recognised. The Governments of Canada and British Columbia reached a final agreement in 1999, following 113 years of negotiation, that recognised the collective ownership by the Nisga'a people of nearly 2000 square kilometres of the Nass River Valley. But even now the United Kingdom, while accepting the concept of collective title to land in its international treaty obligations, interprets this as 'an individual right that may be exercised collectively' not as common or collective property. We continue to attempt to impose a regime of private ownership in spite of legal judgements and treaty rights that are based in the concept of common property rights.

Australia

In Australia the aboriginal population was excluded from the land ownership system imported by the British in 1788. The law held that the country had previously been 'terra nullius' and that the aboriginal peoples had no claim to it. In recent decades steps have been taken to provide some compensation for this. In the Northern Territories and South Australia large tracts of land have been handed back to aboriginal claimants and aboriginal land councils. And in 1993 the Native Land Act, which followed the historic Mabo judgement in the high court the previous year, recognised that 'native title' to land had survived the imposition of a new land tenure system by the British and could be claimed – at least in areas of unused state-owned land. Large areas of Australia are held on 'pastoral leases' and in 1996 the Australian high court in its Wik judgement extended 'native title' to areas in which pastoral leases are held, albeit with pastoral leases taking precedence when the two systems are in conflict (Economist 6/12/97).

Stewardship economy

Stewardship is an attempt to retain the economic benefits of private property rights without losing the social solidarity provided by common ownership. The introduction of stewardship could pose an unintended threat to indigenous peoples who have never suffered the loss that arises from the introduction of private property. Such peoples should be encouraged to retain common or collective title to their land and opt out of the arrangements of a stewardship economy.

Oceans

Private property rights in the oceans have been established much more recently than the ownership of the land. Fishermen have traditionally resisted 'outsiders' working their fishing grounds but the first recognised claim on ocean territory, limited to three miles from the national coastline, was established in 1822 by the North Sea Fisheries Convention that was signed in the Hague by France, Germany, the Netherlands, Denmark and Britain.

Questions of ownership were initially restricted to fishing rights, but this issue became even more pressing when sea-bed deposits of oil, gas and minerals acquired economic importance. In 1945 the United States asserted the right to control mineral resources on its continental shelf. Iceland, followed by other nations, extended its three mile limit progressively to 200 miles between 1950 and 1975 (Mark Kurlansky 1997).

The 1982 UN Law of the Sea Convention now covers most uses of the seas, including fisheries, mining and waste disposal. It allows governments to lay claim to an economic exclusion zone of 200 nautical miles or beyond, if they can demonstrate that the area is an extension of their continental shelf (Donald Denman 1984:32).

Property rights in the oceans have therefore been established within living memory both by unilateral action by a state, often backed by force or the threat of force, and by international agreements. This is a missed opportunity! A system akin to stewardship for the oceans could have been introduced, based on the principles of Paine and Henry George. It was, after all, well after Thomas Paine's 'Agrarian Justice' that the three-mile fishing limit was first agreed in the North Sea, and a century after Henry George's *Progress and Poverty* that more extensive ownership rights were negotiated.

Stewardship of the oceans would provide the same security of tenure needed for the exploitation of mineral resources and the sustainable development of fisheries as is provided by the current regime. But it would share the wealth of the oceans, in the form of their market rent, with a much wider group of nations.

Even more importantly the Law of the Sea leaves the property rights to many areas still contested and has not even been ratified by the USA. Russia, Canada and Denmark all lay claim to much of the Arctic ocean on the grounds that their seabed is continuous with their continental shelves. This is an important source of dispute as the area is a potentially rich source of oil and gas, which is becoming easier to exploit as the polar icecap melts. Indeed, climate change has already progressed far enough for the fabled North East passage to have been taken by commercial shipping for the first time in 2009, shortening the route from the Far East to

Europe via the Suez Canal by 4000 nautical miles and saving $90,000 per ship in fuel costs. The stakes are high and the opportunity for future conflict substantial.

To summarise: These limited examples remind us that ownership is based on historical entitlement, and when the history is examined, there is usually evidence of some discontinuity during which ownership was transferred by violence, royal fiat or trickery.

There are some areas of territory, particularly seabed adjacent to a continental shelf or small islands, where ownership has even now failed to resolve the question of who holds secure property rights. These areas are likely to provide the focus for future conflict.

Stewardship offers a property system in which possession is based not on history but on the willingness of the present steward to compensate those excluded from their land. Not only is it not rooted in coercion, but it also reduces the risk of future conflict and provides a new approach to resolving territorial conflicts (Julian Pratt 2017: 3).

'And then the Earth was not made to be the successive inheritance of children of murderers, that had the strongest arm of flesh, and the best sword .... But it was made for all by the Law of righteousness, and he gives the whole Earth to be the inheritance of every single branch of mankind without respect of person' (Gerrard Winstanley 1649:11)

Chapter 6   Development of economic thinking

The intellectual discipline of economics is built on the concept of ownership on which markets and its price mechanism, generally accepted by orthodox economists. The exception has been Karl Marx and the Marxian school of economics, who challenged the whole edifice of private property and advocated its replacement by collective property. Heterodox (as opposed to orthodox) thinking about property rights in the natural world, to which *Stewardship Economy: Private Property without Private Ownership* contributes, originated in the 18th century with the agrarian radicals like Tom Paine and can be traced though writers from Henry George to Hillel Steiner and the left-libertarians. This tradition makes a clear distinction between artefacts and the natural world.

With the development towards the end of the 20th century of environmental economics, ecological economics and geographical economics, orthodox economists have begun to acknowledge that land and the environment need to be distinguished from artefacts.

The first thinkers to give serious theoretical consideration to the workings of the whole economy were the **Physiocrats** in 18th century France. Their most prominent member, François Quesnay, held that the wealth of a nation derived from the net product of agricultural work on the land – the output minus the inputs, that is to say, the ground rent (François Quesnay 1758/1894). He advocated good husbandry, a tax on landowners equal to the ground rent (l'impôt unique) and the removal of all other taxes (François Quesnay 1760/1846).

Anne-Robert-Jaques Turgot diverged somewhat from this view, believing in the need to foster trade and industry as well as agriculture. But he, too, advocated the removal of taxes such as excise duties and payroll taxes that fell most heavily on the poor while raising taxes on the value of land – particularly previously exempt land belonging to the aristocracy and clergy (Anne-Robert Jaques Turgot 1766/1783: Section 99).

The **classical economists**, who dominated mainstream economic thinking from the 1770s to the 1870s, included Adam Smith, Thomas Malthus, David Ricardo, Thomas Paine, John Stuart Mill and Henry George. They were interested in the overall behaviour of the economy and, in particular, the way that the decisions taken by individuals shaped the functioning of the economy as a whole and the capacity of the economy to grow. They were concerned about the limited amount of land and natural resources available to support the population and its growth.

Classical economists found it easy to make a fundamental distinction between the natural world and artefacts. This was in part due to the importance of the agricultural sector of the economy in the eighteenth and early nineteenth centuries, but also because at that time people found it relatively easy to distinguish between things they thought of as created by God or provided by nature and things produced by people.

In 1771 the Corporation of Newcastle-upon-Tyne enclosed 89 acres of the Town Moor and rented it to developers. The Freemen of the city, who held common property rights to the land, took the Corporation to the assizes where it was determined that Corporation should retain possession but that the rent should be divided amongst the Freemen (Thomas Evans 1821:1).

Thomas Spence (1750-1814) was a self-educated schoolteacher from Scottish Calvinist stock and with a fierce sense of injustice in the world. He was elected in 1775 to the newly formed Newcastle Philosophical Society and presented a lecture on 8th November that year (Thomas Spence 1775b). He was inspired by the finding of the assizes that the Freemen each had an equal right to the rent of the enclosed land. His underlying belief, which he pursued for the rest of his life, is summarised in one of the articles of his *Constitution of a perfect commonwealth*:

'All human beings are equal by nature, and before the law, and have a continual and *inalienable property in the earth*, and its natural production'(Thomas Spence 1798).

78

He believed that property in land was, in a state of nature, held in common and succinctly summarised his Plan to return land to common ownership in a note to his *Essay on Printing*:

'It consists of transferring all the land, waters, mines, houses, and all permanent feudal property to the people, to be held in partnership, and administered for the common benefit, as follows. Each parish or other small district to be the proprietary of that part of the national estate within its boundary, as a body corporate. A board or committee to be appointed by the inhabitants, to let this property on leases only ... These parish or other district boards or committees to receive the rents; and, after deducting their share of the governmental expenses, and all parish and other charges, to make a dividend of the balance remaining to all the people having settlement in the parish or district, as the profit arising from their natural estate'. (Thomas Spence: 1816:5)

Thomas Spence's underlying belief, and his practical proposal, are very similar to stewardship. Even at the outset, however, he suggested that houses along with the natural world should be held by the parish and rented out and his parish-based system provides little opportunity for redistributing the rent on a larger scale. He rapidly developed an antagonism towards landowners, probably exacerbated by his expulsion from the Philosophical Society for publishing the lecture as a broadsheet and by the closure of his school necessitated by landowners withdrawing their children. He advocated the immediate transfer of land to the parish, by force if necessary.

William Ogilvie (1736 – 1813), a scholar and tutor born in Scotland, considered that Natural Law provided that 'every man has a right to an equal share of the soil, in its original state' (1781 or 17822). This arises from a prior state of common ownership: 'The earth having been given to mankind in common occupancy, each individual seems to have by nature a right to possess and cultivate an equal share...No individual can derive from this general right of occupancy a title to any more than an equal share of the soil of his country... It is a birthright which every citizen still retains.' (1781 or 17822)

He was equally clear that those who had improved the land had a right to the additional produce arising from this improvement. In practice this could be achieved by the application of a tax on the unimproved value of land: 'If the original value of the soil be the joint property of the community, no scheme of taxation can be so equitable as a land-tax, by which alone the expenses of the State ought to be supported.' (note 4)

Thomas Paine (1737 -1809) made particularly clear the distinction between 'natural property' (which I describe in this book as the 'natural world') and 'artificial property' (which I describe as 'artefacts'). 'There are two kinds of property. Firstly, natural property, or that which comes to us from the Creator of the universe - such as the earth, air, water. Secondly, artificial or acquired property - the invention of men. In the latter, equality is impossible; for to distribute it equally it would be necessary that all should have contributed in the same proportion, which can never be the case; and this being the case, every individual would hold on to his own property, as his right share. Equality of natural property is the subject of this little essay. Every individual in the world is born therein with legitimate claims on a certain kind of property, or its equivalent' (Thomas Paine 1797b:2)

He accepted that this 'legitimate claim' could not involve the redistribution of land, which would be neither possible nor desirable, and concluded that: 'Every proprietor therefore of cultivated land, owes to the community a *ground–rent*; for I know no better term to express the idea by, for the land which he holds; and it is from this ground rent that the fund proposed in this plan is to issue' (Thomas Paine 1797a:4).

The fund was to be distributed to everyone as a right: 'It is not charity but a right, not bounty but justice, that I am pleading for' (Thomas Paine 1797a: 10).

The key to his approach is the refusal to treat land as the same as man-made goods. This allowed him simultaneously to hold an egalitarian view of property rights to the natural world and a libertarian view of private property in artefacts. 'Whilst, therefore, I advocate the right, and interest myself in the hard case of all those who have been thrown out of their natural inheritance by the

80

introduction of the system of landed property, I equally defend the right of the possessor to the part which is his' (Thomas Paine 1797a: 14). ('the part which is his' here refers to artefacts, and particularly to buildings and improvements).

Stewardship fees are very similar to Paine's proposal to collect the ground rent, although his focus on 'cultivated land' reflects the dominance of agriculture in the creation of wealth in his day.

John Cunliffe (Peter Vallentyne & Hillel Steiner 2000: 3) identifies two **19th century 'liberal-socialists'**, Hyppolyte de Colins and François Huet.

Hippolyte de Colins (1783-1859) (1835 Volume II: 136-155/2000a:125) asserted that humankind has the right to common property of the land. He imagined that once the public was the proprietor of the land (perhaps as a result of bequests by landowners), plots would be rented to the highest bidder for a specified period of time. The rent would then be used for the public good. While he believed that the producer should fully own the product of their labour, his terminology shifts from 'land' to 'immovable property' and suggests that gifts and bequests should also be taxed.

François Huet (1814-1869), a Christian Socialist and Professor of Philosophy at the University of Ghent, (1853 Book III Chapter 7/2000a:107) imagined castaways on a deserted but previously inhabited desert island and suggested that they would organise their property rights by dividing the island into equal shares. He rejected the distinction between the natural world and artefacts, and instead distinguished between things that a person had themself made and things (artefacts and the natural world) that they had inherited from previous generations. Each person is entitled to an equal share of this patrimony and share this right with future generations. This means that the form of property rights to the patrimony are not the same as the property rights to the products of one's labour. His practical proposal was that the portions of the patrimony that become available as a result of death in each year are divided between the young people who reach the age of majority (part at age 14 and the rest at age 25). As the whole of the wealth of the natural world, indeed the whole of the patrimony, is distributed in this way, François Huet's proposal requires a proportional income tax to fund necessary government expenditure.

Left-libertarians

The left-libertarian tradition is identified with the philosophy of Hillel Steiner (1942 -) and is often traced back to the agrarian radicals by way of Henry George and Tom Paine. Left-libertarians hold that where the supply of land is limited, each person can claim only an equal share of its value.

John Cunliffe (Peter Vallentyne & Hillel Steiner 2000: 4) identifies four 19th century 'left-liberals' who firmly advocated private ownership of artefacts and entirely different arrangements for natural resources – Patrick Dove, John Stuart Mill, Herbert Spencer and Henry George. This tradition has been developed in the twentieth century by a number of writers, Hillel Steiner.

The fundamental axiom of **Patrick Edward Dove** (1815 – 1873) was that the creator of an object possesses that object. He argues that all, whether men recognise God as creator or not, have an equal right to the natural world and that the earth can be equitably allocated by making the 'rent-value' of the natural world common property. This rent-value is the only legitimate basis of taxation and should replace all taxes. The allocation of land, and the determination of rents, would be agreed by putting land up for auction from time to time. (page 147 of Vallentyne & Steiner).

John Stuart Mill (1806-1873) differentiated between the natural world and artefacts: 'When the "sacredness of property" is talked about, it should always be remembered, that this sacredness does not belong in the same degree to landed property. No man made the land. It is the original inheritance of the whole species. Public reasons exist for it being appropriated … It is no hardship to anyone, to be excluded from what others have produced… But it is some hardship to be born into the world and to find all nature's gifts previously engrossed, and no place left for the newcomer.' (1848 Book II Chapter II Section 6:272)

He insisted that everybody should bear a fair share of the burden of taxation, by which he meant that 'whatever sacrifices it requires from them should be made to bear as nearly as possible with the same pressure upon all' (1848 Book V Chapter II: 348), which led him to advocate a mix of taxes. However, he made an exception to this equality of sacrifice for taxes on land: 'The ordinary progress of a society which increases in wealth, is at all times tending to augment the incomes of landlords .... independently of any trouble or outlay incurred by themselves. They grow richer, as it were in their sleep, without working, risking, economizing. What claim have they, on the general principle of social justice, to this accession of riches? In what would they have been wronged if society had, from the beginning, reserved a right of taxing the spontaneous increase of rent, to the highest amount required by financial exigencies?' (John Stuart Mill 1848 Book V Chapter 2 Section 5: 360)

Herbert Spencer (1820-1903), English philosopher and anthropologist, advocated in *Social Statics* (1851) that the land should be jointly owned by society. He recognised that if landowners have a valid right to the whole of the earth's surface, everybody else can exist only by consent of the landowners. Starting from the proposition that each person 'has freedom to do all that he wills, provided he infringes not the equal freedom of any other man' (Herbert Spencer 1851 Chapter 8 section 1), he concluded that equity does not permit land ownership. He favoured equality of opportunity rather than equality of reward. Rather than socialism or communism, he proposed: 'a change of landlords. Separate ownerships would merge into the joint-stock ownership of the public. Instead of being in the possession of individuals, the country would be held by the great corporate body – Society. Instead of leasing his acres from an isolated proprietor, the farmer would lease them from the nation' (Herbert Spencer 1851 Part II Chapter IX).

Like Thomas Spence and Herbert Spencer, **Henry George** (1839-1897) advocated collecting the market rent of land and using the revenue for the common good. Like Thomas Spence he believed that it would be fair to abolish all private titles at one stroke. But he proposed a different approach that he believed would be simpler, easier and quieter – to appropriate rent by taxation. This would avoid the disruption of a change in title and either the injustice of confiscating land or the expense of compensating owners for it (Henry George 1879 Book VIII Chapter II:364).

His other great contribution was to insist that something close to the whole of the market rent should be collected for the common good. By advocating an immediate introduction of a tax at close to 100 per cent of market rent, he was effectively advocating confiscation of the whole value of the land (though not of improvements).

Hillel Steiner has argued from first principles in his influential *An essay on rights* (Hillel Steiner 1994) that people have the right to appropriate only an equal portion of unowned things like the natural world.

Liberals

Liberals share the desire for a society in which all individuals can be truly free. The nature of this freedom, or liberty, is what divides them. 'Classical (19th century) liberals' like Adam Smith, David Ricardo and their followers such as Friedrich Hayek and Milton Friedman stressed that liberty is rooted in economic freedom, in particular private property and the freedom from government intervention.

This version of liberty was described by Isaiah Berlin in his famous lecture *Two concepts of liberty* (https://plato.stanford.edu/entries/liberty-positive-negative/#TwoConLib) as 'negative liberty', which he contrasted with 'positive liberty'. For 'social liberals' from John Stuart Mill onwards, most notably John Rawls, freedom is not just the negative liberty of 'freedom from' but the positive liberty of 'freedom to'. They, too, favoured economic freedom, but as a means to a wider freedom that maximises the opportunities of the least advantaged members of society to pursue a reasonable conception of the good. Social liberals advocate positive liberty, with the reduction in inequalities this requires, and view negative liberty as little more than freedom to starve in the gutter.

Drawing on the geo-classical insights of Adam Smith, David Ricardo and Henry George, Gavin Kerr suggests that inequalities can be reduced while expanding economic freedom by developing a new conception of economic freedom in which there is a strengthened and unconditional right to artefacts and the products of human endeavour while property rights to land and the natural world should be conditional on the payment of rent to the community. By insisting on the difference between artefacts and the natural world he reconciles economic and social liberalism (Gavin Kerr 2017).

Collective property

Karl Marx acknowledged the importance of property in land. The Communist Manifesto contains a list of ten measures designed to enable the proletariat 'to wrest, by degrees, all capital from the bourgeoisie, to centralise all the instruments of production in the hands of the State' (Marx & Engels 1848:104).

The first of these measures is the 'Abolition of property in land and application of all rents of land to public purposes.' (Marx & Engels 1848:104). Marx' preferred mechanism for applying the 'rents of land to public purposes' was the collectivisation or nationalisation of land (ref), though this was but a small element of his proposal. In the main body of his writings, Marx rejected the classical distinction between land and capital while still emphasising the importance of property. He developed his attack on the 'trinity formula' (land, labour and capital) in *Capital*. 'Using the very words of political economy we have demonstrated that... the distinction between capitalist and landlord, and that between peasant and industrial worker disappears and the whole of society must fall apart into the two classes of the property owners and the propertyless workers' (Karl Marx 1844: 85).

The labour theory of value led Marx to appear to assert that the natural world, such as agricultural land, does not contribute to the value of the product. 'Land, for example, takes part as an agent of production in creating a use-value, a material product, wheat. But it has nothing to do with the production of the value of wheat. In so far as value is represented by wheat, the latter is merely considered as a definite quantity of materialised social labour, regardless of the particular substance in which this labour is manifested or of the particular use-value of this substance. This nowise contradicts that other circumstances being equal, the cheapness or dearness of wheat depends on the productivity of the soil (Karl Marx K 1894/ 2000 Vol III: 532).' Taking a historical approach he was, however, aware of the underlying importance of land ownership: 'We have seen that the expropriation of the masses of the people from the land forms the basis of the capitalist method of production (Karl Marx, 1867:852 – last 2 chapters).' and went some way towards integrating Ricardo's theory of rent: 'Just as the operating capitalist pumps surplus labour, and thereby surplus value and surplus product in the form of profit, out of the labourer, so the landlord in turn pumps a proportion of the surplus value, or surplus product, out of the capitalist in the form of rent in accordance with the laws already elaborated'. (McLellan 2000:535 and Marx 1894 Book 111 Part VI

The authors of the **Gotha programme** claimed that 'labour is the source of all wealth and all culture' (ref). Karl Marx wrote his 'Critique of the 'Gotha programme' during the last decade of his life – after the publication of Volume I of Das Capital and after writing most of the material published posthumously as Volumes II and II. It can therefore be considered to be a mature and focused expression of his thought. In it he distinguished between 'nature' and capital: 'Labour is *not the source* of all wealth. *Nature* is just as much the source of use values (and it is surely of such that material wealth consists) as is labour... In present-day society, the instruments of labour are the monopoly of the landowners (the monopoly of property in land is even the basis of the monopoly of capital) *and* the capitalists.' (Marx 1875).

There is a clear similarity between his manifesto call for the 'application of all rents of land to public purposes' and Henry George's claim that 'revenues of the common property, land, ought to be appropriated to the common service' (Henry George 1879 Book VIII Chapter IV:380). However, he could not fail to recognise the difference between the nationalisation of land and taxation of its market rent and dismissed Henry George as 'the capitalists' last ditch' (Henry Hyndman 1911 : 281).

In spite of these insights into the importance of land in production, one of Marx's legacies has been to reinforce the view that land is just a form of capital.

The **Fabian Society,** founded in 1884, has always been committed to gradual rather than revolutionary change. But the early Fabians called for the nationalisation of land.

Neoclassical economists

Neoclassical economics, which dominated mainstream economic thinking after the 1870s, focused on the detailed functioning of the economy, what came to be known as microeconomics. It uses the model of equilibrium between supply and demand and the analysis of marginal changes to understand the role of the price mechanism in guiding the decisions of producers and consumers who maximise their individual utilities.

Like Karl Marx, the neoclassical economists were strongly influenced by the intensification of industrialisation, and generally thought of land as just one sort of capital. Their models were therefore two-factor models (capital and labour). It is nowadays difficult for anybody trained in microeconomics to think of land as a separate factor of production.

Mason Gaffney (1994:39) provides evidence from the early neoclassical economists, particularly the founders of the Chicago school, that their two-factor approach was not developed in isolation but with the purpose of countering the ideas of Henry George, which were receiving widespread popular support at the time.

Léon Walras (1834-1910) made a major contribution to neoclassical economics by setting out the general equilibrium theory. He believed that every person has an equal right to the natural world. The land should not belong to all people of one generation, but to all generations – to humanity. In practice this would be achieved if the state owned the natural world, and its receipt of rents would allow the abolition of taxes. (Léon Walras 1896).

Chicago school [text missing]

John Maynard Keynes

With the Depression in the 1920s and 1930s the focus of concern moved back to the functioning of the economy as a whole - macroeconomics. John Maynard Keynes argued that even if an economy were to reach equilibrium, this might be at a level of activity that is associated with involuntary unemployment and that government has a responsibility to manage the overall level of demand in the economy in order to maintain full employment. He believed that land had become insignificant as a factor of production since the industrial revolution. (Keynes 1936:241).

Austrian school

The Austrian school of economists, from Carl Menger through Ludwig von Mises and Friedrich Hayek to Murray Rothbart, have emphasised the positive role of the individual in the economy and the negative role of government intervention. They have been powerful advocates of private property rights and make no distinction between natural property and artefacts. They are also antagonistic towards taxation in any form, and view charges on land and the natural world as just as pernicious as taxes on income: 'Among the specially farsighted is the original pioneer – the man who first found a new site and acquired ownership. Furthermore, in the act of clearing the site, fencing it, and the like, the pioneer inextricably mixes his labor with the original land. Confiscation of land would not only retroactively rob heroic men who cleared the wilderness, it would completely discourage any further pioneering efforts. Why should anyone find new sites and bring them into use when the gain will be confiscated? And how moral is this confiscation? (Murray Rothbard 1957:8). Here again there is no distinction between the natural world and artefacts.

Environmental economics

The concern of the classical economists, that the natural environment would set limits to economic growth, resurfaced in the

1950s. The focus of concern this time was not principally population growth or the amount of available land but pollution and the depletion of non-renewable resources.

Environmental issues had been acknowledged by neoclassical economists but for a long time were not regarded as of central importance. In the 1950s the research organisation, Resources for the Future, was set up in Washington DC to address issues of environmental and resource economics. The group developed economic tools for thinking about the regulation of pollution, emissions permits and resource scarcity.

The first report by the Club of Rome, *The Limits to Growth* (Dennis Meadows 1972), came from outside the discipline of mainstream economics and stimulated widespread debate. It popularised concerns about the allocation and use of natural resources for almost the first time in a century. *The Limits to Growth* described a System Dynamics computer model representing stocks and flows of resources and pollution. Extrapolating contemporary trends and making a number of assumptions about, for example, the quantities of undiscovered resources and rates of population growth led to a number of quite different scenarios, several of which were reminiscent of the concerns of the classical economists - in particular Thomas Malthus' sudden economic collapse and John Stuart Mill's economic stagnation in an ugly and polluted world. The model also suggested that by altering some behaviours immediately the environment could be 'sustainable far into the future' (Dennis Meadows 1972:165). *The Limits to Growth* has been widely criticised, particularly for its aggregate nature and failure to model the price mechanism. However, its business-as-usual scenario (the 'standard run') compares favourably with following 30 years of historical data (as well as predicting a collapse of the global system mid-21st century) (Graham Turner 2008:412). Most importantly, it helped to put environmental issues, including resource depletion and environmental damage, back on the agenda.

Environmental and resource economists suggest that environmental degradation is caused not by economic growth in itself but by distortions that shape economic activity in an inappropriate way.

The most significant is the way in which important costs (like pollution) are externalised from companies' balance sheets, giving rise to distorted prices and unsustainable behaviours.

Environmental economics provides ways to bring these benefits and costs into business and national accounts, for example by selling tradable permits to emit pollution and extract resources from the environment. These put a price on externalities, and environmental economics has brought the issues of property rights and ownership of the environment back into mainstream economics. It offers the opportunity to restructure the pattern of economic activity so that rational economic choices lead to sustainable levels of resource use and pollution. And the sort of property rights it advocates can generally be recognised to be forms of stewardship, in that they require the person holding them to pay a charge for the use of a resource that may be as much as the market rent of the resource (the resource rent).

Geographical economics

The simplifying assumption that land is homogenous has had a corrosive effect on microeconomics since its inception, but geographical economics has gradually restored to economics the importance of location. In spite of the theory of perfect competition in which all firms face the same costs in the long run, costs are in reality unavoidably different at different locations because of differences in market rent at different sites (Brian Hodgkinson 2008:31. Indeed land is frequently an important source of a business monopoly (for example a port) or an oligopoly (for example a small number of supermarket chains). This geographical awareness leads to the realisation that land cannot be treated simply as a form of capital.

The earth cannot be owned

The Earth as divine

Many cultures have treated the Earth as divine, as an entity with a life and a power of her own. Joseph Campbell traces the impact of the Judaeo-Christian tradition:

'Our story of the Fall in the Garden sees nature as corrupt; and that myth corrupts the whole world for us. Because nature is thought of as corrupt, every spontaneous act is sinful and must not be yielded to. You get a totally different civilisation and a totally different way of living according to whether your myth presents nature as fallen or whether nature is in itself a manifestation of divinity, and the spirit is the revelation of the divinity that is inherent in nature' (Joseph Campbell 1988).

In Europe the enclosure of common land took place at the same time as the destruction of the Goddess religion. As the God in heaven replaced the Goddess of the Earth it became easier to objectify and own the land, and as the common lands and forests were enclosed it became more difficult to perform the appropriate ceremonies (Starhawk 1982). But as people have become more open to other world views, this objectification and separation has been challenged.

In 1854 Chief Seattle sold tribal land to the United States government. Since 1971 the words attributed to him by a Hollywood screen writer, Ted Perry (Matt Ridley 1996:214), have found widespread resonance: 'The President in Washington sends word that he wishes to buy our land. But how can you buy or sell the sky? The land? The idea is strange to us. If we do not own the freshness of the air and the sparkle of the water, how can you buy them?

'Every part of the earth is sacred to my people. Every shining pine needle, every sandy shore, every mist in the dark woods, every meadow, every humming insect. All are holy in the memory and experience of my people. We know the sap that courses through the trees as we know the blood that courses through our veins. We are part of the earth and it is part of us. The perfumed flowers are our sisters. The bear, the deer, the great eagle, these are our brothers. The rocky crests, the dew in the meadow, the body heat of the pony, and man, all belong to the same family.

The shining water that moves in the streams and rivers is not just water, but the blood of our ancestors. If we sell you our land, you must remember that it is sacred. Each ghostly reflection in the clear waters of the lakes tells of events and memories in the life of my people. The water's murmur is the voice of my father's father. The rivers are our brothers. They quench our thirst. They carry our canoes and feed our children. So, you must give to the rivers the kindness you would give to any brother.

If we sell you our land, remember that the air is precious to us, that the air shares its spirit with all the life that it supports. The wind that gave our grandfather his first breath also receives his last sigh. The wind also gives our children the spirit of life. So, if we sell you our land, you must keep it apart and sacred, as a place where man can go to taste the wind that is sweetened by the meadow flowers. Will you teach your children what we have taught our children? That the earth is our mother? What befalls the earth befalls all the sons of the earth.

This we know: the earth does not belong to man; man belongs to the earth. All things are connected like the blood that unites us all. Man did not weave the web of life; he is merely a strand in it. Whatever he does to the web, he does to himself. One thing we know: our god is also your god. The earth is precious to him and to harm the earth is to heap contempt on its creator.

Your destiny is a mystery to us. What will happen when the buffalo are all slaughtered? The wild horses tamed? What will happen when the secret corners of the forest are heavy with the scent of many men and the view of the ripe hills is blotted by talking wires? Where will the thicket be? Gone! Where will the eagle be? Gone! And what is it to say goodbye to the swift pony and the hunt? The end of living and the beginning of survival. When the last Red Man has vanished with his wilderness and his memory is only the shadow of a cloud moving across the prairie, will these shores and forests still be here? Will there be any of the spirit of my people left?

We love this earth as a new-born loves its mother's heartbeat. So, if we sell you our land, love it as we have loved it. Care for it as we have cared for it. Hold in your mind the memory of the land as it is when you receive it. Preserve the land for all children and love it, as God loves us all. As we are part of the land, you too are part of the land. This earth is precious to us. It is also precious to you. One thing we know: there is only one God. No man, be he Red

Man or White Man, can be apart. We are brothers after all'.
http://www.csun.edu/~vcpsy00h/seattle.html

This awakening reverence for the earth inevitably makes it difficult to claim to 'own' it and treat it like an artefact.

Gaia

For the last 400 years, the dominant paradigm that has guided our relationship with the earth has viewed the natural world as a complicated machine whose behaviour can be understood by understanding the behaviour of its constituent parts.

'In the sixteenth and seventeenth centuries the mediaeval worldview, based on an Aristotelian philosophy and Christian theology, changed radically. The notion of an organic, living, and spiritual universe was replaced by that of the world as a machine, and the world-machine became the dominant metaphor of the modern era (Frijof Capra 1996:19).'

The success of this paradigm in enabling us to control our environment has reinforced a belief in the underlying metaphor. And if the natural world is no more than a machine, surely it is quite appropriate for us to own it and dispose of it just like any machine of our own making?

An alternative paradigm is to view the natural world as a living system with behaviours that are emergent properties arising from the connections and relationships between the parts (Frijof Capra 1996:5). According to this view, the natural world is not a machine 'out there' for us to understand, own and control.

Science itself is throwing up challenges to the metaphor of the earth as machine. People have been deeply affected by the image of the Earth from the Apollo spacecraft, which has become a symbol for an improbably beautiful, dynamic and vulnerable planet adrift in the darkness. And growing evidence for the Earth's homeostatic mechanisms led James Lovelock to propose the Gaia Hypothesis – the suggestion that the Earth meets the criteria for being a living organism (1979).

We are part of a system, a web of interconnected networks. Our role is to play our part in this complex system. From this perspective we can only play the role of stewards. The natural, living, world cannot be owned.

Greens

Perhaps the most radical challenge to ownership of the natural world comes from Greens. They keep reminding us that human society, including its economy, is entirely dependent on the integrity of natural ecosystems. Greens have a reverence for the natural world, and a sense of wonder at the complexity of the organisation of living systems. Greens give attention to the ecosystem as a whole. They recognise that all the elements of the ecosystem, and their interconnections, are important. So, they recognise homo sapiens as just one of many species on this earth, albeit a very powerful one.

Whereas an environmental economist values the environment as the sum of the values placed on it by all people, Greens recognise the intrinsic value of all species and of the ecosystem as a whole. Greens may find it difficult to accept the category of artefacts as different from that of the rest of the natural world – artefacts are made by people, and we are just another species. But most greens go along with the distinction between artefacts and the natural world for instrumental reasons. It provides a way of putting some limits on the right that many people claim to do what they want with the natural world.

Fritz Schumacher advocated, on both ethical and pragmatic grounds, a new way of thinking about ownership of the natural world. 'Man has not made (land and the creatures upon it), and it is irrational for him to treat things that he has not made and cannot recreate once he has spoilt them, in the same manner and spirit as he is entitled to treat things of his own making.' (E F Schumacher 1973:88)'

Aldo Leopold recognised the problems caused by ownership of the natural world: 'Conservation is getting nowhere because it is incompatible with our Abrahamic concept of land. We abuse land because we regard it as a commodity belonging to us. When we

94

see land as a community to which we belong, we may begin to use it with love and respect. There is no other way for land to survive the impact of mechanised man, nor for us to reap from it the esthetic harvest it is capable, under science, of contributing to culture.' (Aldo Leopold 1948/1976: viii)

He argued for a new land ethic 'When god-like Odysseus returned from the wars in Troy, he hanged all on one rope a dozen slave-girls of his household whom he suspected of misbehaviour during his absence. This hanging involved no question of propriety. The girls were property. The disposal of property was then, as now, a matter of expediency, not of right and wrong (Aldo Leopold 1948/1976: 201).

The first ethics dealt with the relations between individuals; the Mosaic Decalogue is an example. Later accretions dealt with the relation between the individual and society(Aldo Leopold 1948/1976: 202).

'There is as yet no ethic relating to man's relation to land and to the animals and plants that grow upon it. Land, like Odysseus' slave-girls, is still property. The land-relation is still strictly economic, entailing privileges but not obligations' (Aldo Leopold 1948/1976: 203).

'Land ultimately cannot be owned by anybody. Land is constant while human life is transient upon it (Herbert Girardet 1976)'.

To summarise: The dominant way of thinking about ownership ensures that the system of property rights to the natural world is the one that has been developed, probably very appropriately, for artefacts. However, this has never been the only view, and the principle of stewardship is not alone amongst contemporary approaches that distinguish artefacts from the natural world.

Over the last 200 years economists have differed about whether to make a distinction between the natural world and things made my people. If no distinction is made, then economics chooses to ignore both geography, in particular the significance of location, and the dependence of economies on finite natural resources that cannot be produced at will. Over the last 50 years there has been a growing acceptance of the distinctiveness of the natural world, the need for sustainable development and the significance of property rights in the natural world.

The mental models that underlie ownership economies make only a very weak distinction between the natural world (land) and artefacts (things made by people). Yet these forms of property right are fundamentally different. The refusal to consider any possible difference between nature and artefacts is a way of undermining our capacity to think about alternatives to the status quo.

Stewardship (Chapter 7) rests on an absolute distinction between the natural world and artefacts.

Chapter 7   Stewardship is fairer than ownership

This chapter brings together material set out earlier in the book to show the inadequacies and unfairness of our familiar form of private property, ownership, and the much greater fairness of stewardship. It foregrounds the framework of duties, rights and goals outlined above (Chapter 3), and uses this to explore the ethical basis for stewardship.

One way of making the case for stewardship is to develop an argument from a particular philosophical perspective. The most thoroughly worked through examples come from the left-libertarian school of Henry George and Hillel Steiner and from the liberal argument articulated by Gavin Kerr (2017).

This chapter does not go back to a single philosophical position but takes a different and more inclusive approach. It briefly sets out the justifications that have been advanced to support an ownership economy, and suggests that all of these, other than those arguing from the special rights of labour and first occupancy, provide an equal or better justification for stewardship than they do for ownership.

Stewardship as alternative to ownership

Stewardship provides a fairer way than does ownership to allocate the natural world to people than does ownership; and it compensates those who are excluded from this access. This claim applies equally to the whole of the natural world including resources, like the atmosphere and the oceans, that have been managed in ownership economies as open access regimes or common property regimes. Stewardship is a way to:

- allocate land in a way that is fair and efficient
- share the benefits of development
- share the risks and burdens of change.

This applies only to a steady-state stewardship economy. Transition from an ownership economy is described in book 2.

A different conception of private property

In a stewardship economy the Land Stewardship Trust holds all the land of the country in trust as common or collective property. It allocates each plot to a steward, who has the right of access and the right to make decisions about its use – that is to say, who has private property rights. The differences between a stewardship economy and an ownership economy may be summarised using A M Honoré's list (Chapter 2) of the features of the liberal conception of private ownership with the differences from ownership highlighted in **bold**:

- **the duty to pay annual stewardship fees**
- the right to possess
- the right to use
- the right to manage (determine how it is used by others)
- the right to the income that can be derived (from permitting others to use it)
- the right to the capital value **of improvements, but not of the land,** at the time of sale
- the right to security (against expropriation)
- the right to transfer it indefinitely by gift or bequest to another
- the absence of any term on the possession of any of these rights
- the prohibition of harmful use
- **the responsibility to care for the land (set out in husbandry clauses)**

- **liability for damage (disimprovement) to their own or to others' land**
- the liability that certain judgements against them may be executed on it
- the expectation that, when the rights of others in the object lapse, those rights will return to him.

This conception of property is compatible with common law and leasehold but would amount to a major challenge in civil law jurisdictions where property rights are nearly as absolute for the natural world as for artefacts.

It is sometimes claimed that stewardship is nationalisation of land in all but name, that the state effectively owns the land, and the individual has use-rights conditional on paying rent. But Honoré's list makes it clear that what is going on is something quite different – that the individual has the right to the capital value of the land and to its usage, but the collective has the right to the rent.

While private stewards hold most of the land in stewardship, at a national level the Land Stewardship Trust holds the property rights. By receiving stewardship fees on behalf of everybody the Trust is holding a common or collective property right over all land.

The security of tenure of a steward is comparable with that of an owner-occupier who has a mortgage on the same property in an ownership economy. Tenure is secure as long as the regular payments (stewardship fees or mortgage repayments) are made. Indeed, if provisions are made for the steward to defer payments as a charge against the value of their building when it is sold, the security of tenure is greater than in an ownership economy.

Stewardship is an alternative to private ownership, but collective property and common property may also be held in stewardship. The collective, or the body of commoners, have to behave as stewards – that is to say they have a shared responsibility to care for the land and a duty to pay stewardship fees to the Land Stewardship Trust.

The rest of this chapter considers some of the topics set out in Honore's list to evaluate how a stewardship economy may be justified against each.

Allocating land

Duties, goals, rights

Can the arguments for private property based in duty, goals and rights, which have been used to seek to justify ownership, also provide a justification for stewardship?

Stewardship is not necessarily compatible with some ideas of duty, like the duty of obedience to a sovereign or state. But it can be thought of and justified as a duty-based property regime in that anybody who makes use of the natural world has a duty to compensate those who are excluded from the steward's land by paying stewardship fees.

Where goals provide the justification for private property, these same goals might just as well justify a well-considered system of common or collective property. On the other hand, goals may justify a variety of different forms of private property such as those in which interests are held only for life, or where the proprietor has the right to use the object in question, but capital value is held by the family. However, these are not the issues here. This chapter is concerned to demonstrate that familiar goal-based theories are as compatible with stewardship as they are with ownership. Stewardship can be thought of as a goal-based system of property rights that supports many aspects of a fair and just society and, in particular, supports the goals of:

- harmony, stability and security
- efficient use of land
- economic efficiency
    - a stewardship economy is based on the use of market mechanisms, improves the efficiency of the

land market and does away with the deadweight loss of taxes

- a stewardship economy provides greater motivation for the individual than an ownership economy, as the whole of 'whatever is produced by man's industry' is 'secured to him' without being subject to taxation
- fairness and equality of opportunity – stewardship guarantees an equal share of the wealth of the natural world for everybody
- sustainability.

A stewardship economy is an obvious contender for the design of a just and fair society under the conditions of a veil of ignorance (Chapter 3) but let us consider another example. Suppose that, in an ownership economy, a farm-owner dies intestate, and her children have to decide what to do with the farm. Suppose also that the brothers and sisters all want to reach a fair settlement. Possible solutions, and drawbacks, might include:

❑ Sell the farm and divide the money. One drawback is that some of the siblings may wish to continue farming the land.

❑ Divide the farm into equal lots. One drawback is that the farm may become less productive if divided.

❑ Farm together as a collective. One drawback is that this might not suit them all.

❑ The one prepared to offer the highest price to buy out the others. One drawback is that, if the buyer has to borrow to pay off the others, the interest payments will make it difficult for the farm to be profitable until inflation has reduced the value of the repayments. By this time the value of the land will have risen, and the others may be regretting having let their share go.

❑ The one prepared to pay the highest *rent* makes use of the farm. The rent is divided equally amongst them all. In this situation the highest bidder will not bid more than the current market rent of the land so will immediately be able to earn a living from the land. If the market rent rises over time, all the brothers and sisters benefit.

We see from the alternative solutions to the dilemma that retaining a shared claim on the market rent while encouraging individual use of the property is fair and workable. A similar mechanism, relating only to land and not including any improvements to that land, and scaled up to the level of the state, provides the model for stewardship. In general terms stewardship reconciles the twin Utilitarian goals of equality (achieved by sharing the rent) with security (by providing security of tenure). It meets Rawls' goal of justice as fairness.

Stewardship can be described as a **general rights-based approach**. The general rights on which it is founded is that everybody has the right to hold private property, and everybody has the right to an equal share of the wealth of the natural world. It is compatible with other general rights-based approaches including **eligibility** and **freedom from expropriation**.

Stewardship is fully compatible with the general right for everybody to own artefacts and to hold a form of private property, stewardship, in land and the natural world.

A stewardship economy acknowledges the general right of all citizens to life. Each individual needs access to the natural world in order to survive. If we can be excluded from the surface of the Earth because it is owned by others we are reduced to the position of slaves, owned by landlords who can set their own terms for access. The minimum right would be to enough land to survive, but the recognition that the Earth is the common heritage of mankind means that we all have the right to an equal share to the wealth of the natural world, This is not a right to ownership of a particular share, but to an equal claim on the market rent of the earth. Kant stated 'We are nature's guests. We all have an equal right to the good things which nature has provided.... God has left men to do the sharing'. (Kant 1781:192)

Stewardship is fully compatible with a general right to freedom from expropriation and security of tenure, but conditional on the payment of stewardship fees. Avoiding expropriation during transition from an ownership economy is discussed below.

Stewardship of the natural world can be described as a **special rights-based theory.** The principle of justice on which it relies, both in acquisition and in transfer, is the payment of a market rent as compensation to others for occupation and use of land. It is rooted in relationships between people in the here and now, not in a historical relationship between a person and a thing.

Stewardship also provides a simple and transparent way to realise the Lockean proviso (Chapter 4). When 'enough, and as good' land is not available, the next best thing is a guaranteed Universal Income, paid by those who have acquired the use of the land and equal to the benefit they derive from holding it. This is enough to rent a fair, equal, share of the land and is an integral part of the property right rather than something provided by a separate tax–benefit system that has been introduced to compensate for the limitations of ownership.

Stewardship is consistent with a version of the labour theory of special rights only as far as artefacts are concerned. It accepts that things that are produced by people, including improvements to land such as houses and fences, belong entirely to their makers to do what they want with. Indeed, in a stewardship economy this 'entirely' is not compromised by the taxation of production and consumption. But stewardship is not compatible with the assertion that a person who improves land thereby gains a special right to ownership of the land itself.

Stewardship is consistent with a very limited version of first occupancy, in that it confers on the first occupier (and those to whom title is subsequently transferred) the stewardship of the land, including security of tenure provided that they continue to pay the stewardship fees. But it does not confer ownership.

It differs from most special rights-based justifications of ownership in the way it treats claims to the market rent of land. Stewardship challenges the assertion that this market rent can be acquired as a special right by an individual, either by labour or first occupancy. It denies that, in an established stewardship economy, people and firms can claim the exclusive use of any land or natural resources without compensating the rest of us on an ongoing basis.

In the end, each of us has to decide whether we find more compelling the 'first come, first served' approach of first occupancy, or the owner's willingness continually to compensate others for excluding them from the natural world.

In a stewardship economy the seats at Cicero's theatre are no longer permanently reserved (and often unoccupied!) by a class of hereditary theatre-goers, but each seat is available to the highest bidder for this year only; and those of us who can't get in are compensated.

The claims of right-libertarian thinkers like Robert Nozick, based in special rights and the denial of any right to a share of subsistence, cannot be reconciled with stewardship. Stewardship does, however, provide a market mechanism for the allocation of land use that seems to sit more comfortably with the rest of the right-libertarian position than does the particular special rights-based approach they have chosen to adopt.

The history of discontinuities caused by conquest and fraud is superseded by an approach grounded in present compensation not past acquisition.

Allocation based in the present

In an ownership economy there is widespread agreement that the answer to the question, 'who has the *present* rights to a piece of territory?' is to be found in the *past* rather than the present. Just as with artefacts we ask the pragmatic questions that form the basis of Roman Law: from whom it was obtained, was it obtained legally and did the previous owner have a good title to ownership? Problems arise with judgements about historical entitlements when there are conflicting claims. This may happen when land is not registered with the Land Registry and the deeds are missing or incomplete. It may happen when someone dies intestate. More importantly it occurs with territories claimed by different states, or minority groups within a state.

Any system that allocates present land rights on the basis of past events must be prepared to examine the full chain of events that have led up to the present allocation of land. It is difficult to imagine that any state will not readily find, in its history, times when land rights have been taken by force from previous owners (Chapter 5).

In addition to its origin in conflict, there will always be uncertainty about historical title to land. The Australian state held until 1992 that Australia, before European settlement, was *terra nullius*, or 'vacant lands'. The grounds for this claim were that the indigenous peoples did not have cultivation or an organised system of land ownership. But since 1992 the colonial system of property rights has been significantly re-assessed (Chapter 5).

How far back into history should the current title to land in Israel-Palestine be traced – 1967, 1948, 1917, two millennia? In the UK do the monastic orders still have a claim to the land confiscated by King Henry VIII? And why accept the right of King William I to wipe the slate clean in 1066? This question of allocation lies at the heart of international territorial disputes and the resultant political and military conflicts.

Property systems based in past events have an unacceptable ultimate basis, that of force. They provide an unacceptable mechanism for resolving present disputes and, by fossilising the present, invite future conflict. The future offers only further opportunities for conflict. We would do better to adopt an ethically acceptable way of allocating *present* land rights in the *present*.

And what of the *future*? If a state tackles an unequal distribution of land ownership within its territory by means of a programme of land reform, how can it prevent subsequent generations from repeating the consolidation of land rights that is the root problem? Beyond the boundaries of individual states, should we be looking for mechanisms that allow their boundaries to be more fluid and negotiable than the rigid boundaries that normally change only as a result of warfare? (Julian Pratt 2017: 9)

Freedom and ownership

One of the major problems with the ownership of land is the way that ownership constrains the freedom of those who do not own land. Philippe Van Parijs (1995:14) highlights this by describing a hypothetical island on which, through an impeccable process of acquisition, one person comes to own all the land. If it is difficult to leave the island, the owner can impose whatever conditions they wish on the other inhabitants and can reduce them to slavery. Even when people have freedom of movement in ownership economies, they cannot move to a place where they can be sure of having access to land.

Stewardship can be thought of as a particular form of private property, though it is also a perfectly appropriate form of common or collective property. It is fully compatible with the general right to own property, and indeed there would probably be more stewards in a stewardship society than there are owners in an ownership society.

Stewardship can be thought of as a duty-based property system – the duty of a steward to compensate others.

Stewardship can be justified on the grounds that it promotes many different goals for an economic system, including those of economic efficiency, economic fairness (Gavin Kerr 2017) and care for the land.

Stewardship rejects the idea that it is possible to base ownership claims on special rights acquired *in the past*, whether this be by first occupancy or by labour. Instead, it is based on the special right that arises when the steward pays *ongoing* compensation to everybody excluded from using the land. This is far more compelling than the special rights on which ownership is based. Stewardship is a more ethical form of private property than ownership.

All of these ethical theories of property provide support for stewardship that is at least as compelling as for ownership and taken together this support is much more compelling.

Land Value Capture

The market rent of a piece of land has nothing to do with the mixing of labour by its owners or its first occupation but is due to competition for land. Market rents rise, in the local area and in society as a whole, as the population grows and its economic activity increases. This market rent should be available to society, not captured by individual owners. This provides a rationale for using some of the income from stewardship fees to fund the economy and society.

This section discusses the determinants of land value and the uplift in land value that takes place when planning restrictions are removed or infrastructure provided.

Determinants of land value

As a community develops in knowledge, technology, production, markets, services, safety and in sheer numbers, competition for desirable land grows and its market rent increases. It is famously recognised, for example, that most of the financial gains from the invention of the air-conditioner went not the inventors or manufacturers but to the owners of land in places like Florida where previously unattractive land became a desirable place to live (ref).

Adam Smith recognised that:

'... every improvement in the circumstances of the society tends either directly or indirectly to raise the real rent of land' (Adam Smith Volume I Part I Chapter XI:374).

Conversely, if the economy of a country or neighbourhood declines then market rents, and market values, will fall.

The rent that a landlord receives for their land depends in complex ways on the wider society – on local issues like:

Restrictions on use
- o planning restrictions
- o easements and covenants

Physical aspects of the site
- o topography, orientation, soil fertility, subsoil, soil pollution, micro-climate
- o liability to flooding.

Physical surroundings
- o light, views, privacy, surrounding properties and the local built environment, street lighting, access to parks, open spaces, river frontage, sea
- o noise, traffic, air pollution, smells.

Social environment
- o population density
- o safety, security
- o social factors that are negative or thought to be negative such as proximity to prisons and psychiatric hospitals
- o cleanliness
- o proximity to employment
- o proximity to shops, sports facilities and cultural sites
- o school catchment area.

Economic environment
- o economic usefulness of the site
- o proximity to similar or related businesses
- o connection to services (water, drainage, sewage, gas, electricity, telephone)
- o access to transport (local roadways, car parking off site, motorway, rail, river, canal, sea)
- o state of the local economy, availability and cost of labour and skills
- o proximity to local markets
- o insurance costs
- o levels of taxation

and on national issues such as:

- o whether the state provides legally enforceable title
- o the general economic climate
- o protection from crime, terrorism, and war.

If crime is low in a particular residential area and it is attractively maintained with clean streets, good street lighting and parks then the market rents of properties are higher – as they are if it is served by good transport links and high quality schools. This insight is used by economists when they want to estimate the amount that people would be willing to pay for one of these public goods. The principle is to identify two locations that are identical in every way apart from the availability of a particular public good; the difference in land values between the two locations is then equal to the value of the public good. The practice is to construct a hedonic pricing model in which many sites are modelled using evidence of their market value (or market rent) and a range of the determinants of land value listed above. Multiple regression analysis is then used to identify the importance of each determinant. Market rents reflect the sum of the benefits received as a result of occupying that particular location.

Advocates of Land Value Taxation since Henry George have argued that the market rent of land should be taxed because it is created by the actions of the community not the actions of the landowner. The owner of an unimproved plot of land in the financial district of capital city will indeed have seen its market rent and market value appreciate by a factor of thousands during the last century as a result of the financial activity taking place on the sites around it, all without any effort on their part. We have heard fiery rhetoric to denounce the role, though not the person, of the landowner – Winston Churchill, a supporter of Land Value Taxation, spoke in support of the People's Budget in 1909: 'Roads are made, streets are made, railway services are improved, ...water is brought from reservoirs a hundred miles off in the mountains - and all the while the landlord sits still... To not one of these improvements does the land monopolist as a land monopolist contribute, and yet by every one of them the value of his land is sensibly enhanced.'

The proposal to capture market rents, and particularly increases in market rent, is compelling. But the term 'unearned increment' may not be helpful. Critics of Land Value Taxation, particularly from the libertarian perspective, point out that income from labour and capital also benefits from the advancement of society – plumbers and lawyers earn more as society advances and greater profits are generated by business.

I do not seek to justify stewardship on the grounds that it arises from the general advancement of society, or that it represents an unearned increment. I suggest simply that stewardship is a fair and economically efficient way to order our property rights in the natural world. And it is reassuring that in a stewardship economy every member of society, not just the fortunate few, benefits from changes which result in increase in the value of land, whether these result from changes in planning regulations, or public investment in infrastructure or services

Planning gain

Planning regulations restrict the construction of buildings for housing, commercial and industrial purposes. This is because the market does not always, or even often, act in the public interest. The purpose of planning varies in different times and places to preserve agricultural land, prevent sprawl or promote national food security. At times it has responded to concern about the financial costs of providing services for a highly dispersed population – transport, utilities, sewage, postal services, health and social care and so on. At times planning has taken account of environmental costs – rural households use more energy than urban ones, and development in rural areas may lead to the loss of habitat and species. And at times it has prevented the loss of countryside as an aesthetic, recreational and spiritual asset.

As the population and the economy has grown, there is often a need to grant planning permission for development on agricultural land. When this happens the value of the land rises by perhaps a hundredfold. In an ownership economy it is the fortunate owner who reaps this windfall. In a stewardship economy we all benefit because the land is allocated to the individual bidding the highest stewardship fees, which are then distributed across the population.

Infrastructure projects

There is a particular issue in the case of new infrastructure projects, for example where a government proposes to build a new commuter rail link. In an ownership economy, those who own land served by the link will see the value of their properties rise. In a stewardship economy the properties that benefit from improved infrastructure pay higher stewardship fees, and the revenue is used to provide self-funding transport infrastructure or to supplement the Universal Income.

Public investment not public spending

Public spending on safety, security, education, health, the arts and many other determinants of land value listed above all increase land value and so increase stewardship fees. This can then be reinvested in providing these community goods. In a stewardship economy the neoliberal narrative that public spending is a drain on the activities of the private sector will fall away as infrastructure and other public goods become self-funding and public spending comes to be seen as rational investment even in narrow economic terms.

Sharing the risks and burdens of change

In an ownership economy the individual landowner benefits from positive changes in the community but also suffers from negative changes in the community that are no fault of their own. In a stewardship economy benefits and risks are shared.

Economic downturn and negative equity

Some people may need to buy a house at a time when market rents, and so land prices, are about to fall, either due to an economic downturn or in that locality. If people have had to take out a loan to buy the house, they may find themselves with negative equity. They may then find themselves unable to move home (for example to obtain work) and saddled with a debt they can't repay. In an economic downturn in a stewardship economy, by contrast, the value of the steward's asset (the building) is protected and there is no risk of negative equity provided revaluations are frequent and ideally on a rolling basis. The steward's monthly expenditure in stewardship fees falls during the downturn. This provides each steward, individual or firm, with some protection from economic hardship although the Universal Income will also fall during a recession.

Disappearing land

In coastal regions, where there is erosion or rising sea levels, land may be lost to the sea or to saltmarsh. In an ownership economy the cost falls on the individual landowner, who feels aggrieved if the state does not make what they consider to be sufficient investment in sea defences. In a stewardship economy the owner still bears the cost of the loss of their improvements (for example, buildings), but not the cost of the loss of their land. The stewardship fees that they have to pay falls – to zero if the land is completely lost to the sea.

Environmental damage

In an ownership economy it is landowners who suffer the financial consequences when the environmental quality of their land is harmed by some external source of pollution, whether this be regular agricultural runoff or a unique event like Windscale, Three Mile Island, Chenobyl or Fukushima.

In a stewardship economy local people are compensated as the stewardship fees fall in the affected area, and we all bear the cost as the Universal Income falls.

Not in my back yard

If a prison, secure hospital or even a major road is planned or built in an ownership economy, the value of adjacent land may fall. It is as though land values are contaminated by developments just as they may be contaminated by pollution. When these sort of developments are made, compensation may be available but may not be – and, even if it is, will usually take the form of a one-off payment. In a stewardship economy, the fall in land value would be borne not by the individual steward, who pays lower stewardship fees, but by everybody equally.

Public demands on the landowner

There are many demands that we make on landowners, including rights of way, maintaining paths and stiles, respecting habitats of newts or bats etc. These reduce the market rent of land in the same way that planning restrictions do. In a stewardship economy such demands cause a fall in the stewardship fees for that property, so it is all of us who bear the financial burden not the individual landowner. Indeed, if demands are stringent the stewardship fees may become negative (stewardship support fees).

Planning restrictions

Just as the lifting of planning restrictions increases the market rent of land, so imposing restrictions reduces the rent. In 2004 the state of Oregon passed Ballot Measure 37; this offered landowners whose land values were reduced by environmental or land use regulations compensation from the state. The measure has been severely modified since then, but it raised the debate about who should bear the cost of planning restrictions. In a stewardship economy, imposing planning restrictions results in the steward paying lower stewardship fees than if they were absent, and we all pay for them as our Universal Income is reduced.

A fee for the right to occupy and use land

Stewardship provides a way to allocate land amongst people and firms on the basis of present willingness to pay the market rent of the land as stewardship fees. The fees are a payment for the use of the land. They reflect the value of the services provided to that land by society, enterprise and the state including the physical and socio-economic aspects of its environment.

In a very different context, the principle behind stewardship offers a way of settling international territorial disputes that are threatening to degenerate into war (Thomas Paine 1802 / 2017).

Intergenerational equity

Intergenerational inequity arises from many aspects of our economy, but one of the most importance is the unequal access of younger people to land when all land is already owned by the older generations. Thomas Jefferson wrote from Paris to James Madison: 'The question, whether one generation of men has right to bind another, seems never to have been started either on this or on our side of the water... I set out on this ground which I suppose to be self-evident, 'that the earth belongs in usufruct to the living;' that the dead shall have neither powers nor rights over it. ...it will exclude, at the threshold of our new government the contagious and ruinous errors of this quarter of the globe, which have armed despots with means not sanctioned by nature for binding in chains their fellow men.' (1789)

A few years earlier, in 1775, Thomas Spence (1775), had developed an answer to Jefferson's question about preventing one generation binding another, through his proposal that the land belongs to the living inhabitants in equal shares.

Ethics of transition to a stewardship economy

The description in *Stewardship Economy: Private Property without Private Ownership* focuses on an ideal steady state. The question of transition from some other economic system is addressed last because it is only worth considering when one is convinced that the steady-state proposal has some merit. Transition to a stewardship economy does not have any single practical course or clear-cut ethical justification, but though it is possible to consider the ethics of particular transition situations (see book 2.).

Rapid introduction of stewardship into an economy where land is in private ownership would amount to confiscation of land value, which would be unethical and unacceptable. Most advocates of the introduction of a Land Value Tax, its equivalent when required by the state, suggest initially introducing the tax at 10 per cent of the market rent of land and gradually increasing the proportion to 90 per cent.

Transition could, on the other hand, be acceptable if, as envisaged by John Stuart Mill, the stewardship fees are equal to any increase in the market rent that occurs after stewardship was introduced. This allows the steward to keep the whole of any property rights that they hold at the onset of transition, and merely asks them to surrender any future increase in the value of those rights. The efficient market hypothesis suggests that these possible future increases are already factored into the value at the onset of transition.

One situation in which rapid transition to a full stewardship economy may be acceptable is where there is consensus within a state that there is a need for land reform. For example, in Eastern Europe in the early 1990s several states wanted to transfer land from state ownership to private ownership. Here, provided that the initial legitimacy of the state ownership was accepted, and other historical claims of land ownership were denied, stewardship could have been introduced rapidly without violating any ethical principle (see book 2).

Comparison with slavery

History and justifications

Slavery was an accepted feature of many ancient cultures, including the Mesopotamian, Indian, Chinese, Egyptian, Hebrew, Greek, Roman, Aztec, Inca and Mayan civilisations. In Europe between the 5th and 10th centuries it was transformed into the less binding system of serfdom, though more than 1 per cent of the inhabitants of England were recorded in Domesday Book as slaves. Slavery was accepted and widespread in both Christian and Islamic lands in the mediaeval period. But it was the exploration of Africa and the colonisation of the Americas in the 16th centuries that led to the modern development of slavery, which is defined as:

'the most absolute involuntary form of human servitude. The definitive characteristics of slaves are as follows: their labour or services are obtained through force; their physical beings are regarded as the property of another person, their owner; and they are entirely subject to their owner's will. Since earliest times slaves have been legally defined as things; therefore, they could, among other possibilities, be bought, sold, traded, given as gifts, or pledged for a debt by their owner, usually without any recourse to personal or legal objection or restraint' (Encarta 97 encyclopaedia).

Aristotle allowed for the enslavement of people belonging to an inferior civilisation, which naturally excluded all Greeks. According to the doctrine of natural slavery, just as tame animals fare better when ruled by man so certain men are of such a nature that they benefit from enslavement. St. Augustine was able to accept slavery on the grounds that it was the consequence of original sin – the same grounds that permitted private ownership of the natural world.

Locke believed that, in general:

'Every man has a property in his own person. Thus, no body has any right but to himself' (John Locke 1690:II 27).

Nevertheless, he embraced the doctrine that slavery was ethically acceptable if the slaves were captured in the course of a 'just war' as slavery was a lesser loss of freedom than being put to death.

Until late in the eighteenth century the ownership of people was widely considered to be morally acceptable. Legal positivism applies the logic of property to people just as to goods – if a given legal system recognises the existence of slavery, then slaves can be owned. Applying this argument to people is on more shaky ground than applying it to artefacts as the relevant law is the law of contract, and it cannot be alleged that slavery is based on voluntary contracts.

The relationship between master and servant used to be determined, however, by a branch of English property law; and although a man did not own his wife her 'conjugal affection' was treated as his property (Alan Ryan 1987: 2). Libertarians generally hold that self-ownership is such a strong principle that it is quite possible to choose to sell oneself into slavery (Robert Nozick 1974:371).

Transition – abolition

Since the beginning of the nineteenth century there has been widespread opposition to slavery on ethical grounds. Hegel argued that slavery involved a conceptual as well as an ethical impropriety –

116

men so thoroughly possess themselves that there is no room for anyone else's possession of them.

The political campaign for the abolition of slavery developed in the 18th and 19th centuries. The abolitionists were long regarded as a radical minority with no respect for the rights of property. But England finally abolished its slave trade in 1807 and emancipated the slaves in its colonies in 1833. The architect of the campaign was the Quaker Thomas Clarkson and its main parliamentary spokesman an Evangelical Christian, William Wilberforce. Their motivation stemmed from a recognition that all human beings are equally deserving of respect – what a Quaker might describe as 'that of God in everyone'. A new understanding of what it is to be human led to a change in the nature of ownership, a recognition that people cannot 'own' other people in the same way that they could own a table or chair. This was not enough, however, for emancipation to be carried through without the payment of large sums to slave-owners as compensation.

Land

Aldo Leopold invited a moral debate and political change of similar magnitude when he called for a new Land Ethic (1949/1968, chapter 6). Over the last half a century there has been a sea-change in the way that people understand our relationship with the earth. It is time, now, to recognise that the earth, too, cannot be owned in the sense that 'ownership' is commonly applied to the natural world. Just as economies were able to flourish after the abolition of slavery, so they will continue to flourish if we make the transition from ownership to stewardship. The sense of outrage at ownership of the natural world could never, of course, be as great as the sense of outrage at slavery - but the acceptance of ownership of the natural world may one day, in a similar way, be regarded as a shameful period in our economic history.

To summarise: stewardship provides a fair way to:

- allocate the natural world among competing users

- ensure that the financial benefits of state investment and the development of civil society accrues to us all, not just to those who own land

- ensure that the costs of negative changes in the environment or society are borne by us all, not by individual landowners.

The justifications for private property that have been mounted to defend ownership are equally or even more cogent in their defence of stewardship. A general right to property exists in both ownership and stewardship economies. The goals that can be achieved by stewardship include those achieved by ownership, and many more besides. The duties in which stewardship is rooted require respect for all people and for the environment. It is far more equitable to grant a special right to property in the natural world on the grounds that the steward compensates, on an ongoing basis, those who are excluded than granting ownership to the first occupiers or those who mix their (or their servants') labour with it.

There are several categories of ownership that have been accepted in the past but are unthinkable now – the particularly shocking example of human slavery. It is time to recognise that ownership of the natural world is also unthinkable.

Chapter 8 Final word on ownership, stewardship and transition

This chapter provides a brief restatement of the case for stewardship on grounds of ethics and efficiency and looks at transition in this light.

The economy rests upon and grows out of society and the ecosystems of the planet. Conflict, poverty, inequalities and environmental degradation need to be viewed in the context of the societal choices that underpin our economies. These include the rule of law, the law of contract and the property system.

We do need secure title to the use-right to plots of land, but this can be provided by stewardship instead of ownership. Stewardship is a secure use-right that brings the associated responsibility to care for the land and the duty to pay a ground rent (the market rent of the land but not any buildings or other improvements) to be used for the benefit of all. As has been explained previously, this revenue would be distributed on an equal per capita basis as a Universal Income instead of any existing benefit system, and a proportion of each person's Universal Income would be used to support collective endeavours through government funding.

The same logic, that stewards should pay rent to be used for the benefit of all, is applied, not just to proprietors of land and the rest of the natural world but, to the holders of other rights that are granted by governments and confer a sole (monopoly) right to conduct some activity such as printing money, intellectual property rights and operating franchises.

Ownership

Ethics

Justifications for ownership

We can rightfully claim to own things that we have created (artefacts), most notably on the grounds both that we have laboured to make them or acquired them through a series of voluntary transaction from whoever did so – John Locke's labour theory of property aligned with Immanuel Kant's emphasis on with the will to possess. But his suggestion that it is possible to claim outright and perpetual ownership of land, in addition to any improvements, by being the first to 'mix one's labour' with the soil is simply not tenable.

The other plank of John Locke's justification, of particular relevance to landed property, is the principle of first occupation. Even in America, where he observed the homesteading model, this could only have been acceptable if the land had previously been unoccupied; and his proviso that 'as much and as good' be left for others certainly has no traction today. The same is true for claims arising from having been the discoverer or first user of the rest of the natural world – the rights to use water, air and minerals.

There are other theories that can also provide justifications for the ownership of land that are more or less convincing, but each of these provides a better justification for the conditional use-right of stewardship than they do for ownership.

We have made a colossal mistake in applying the concept of unconditional and perpetual ownership rights to the natural world, particularly the land. We currently seek to justify ownership of land on the grounds that these property rights are the result of a long series of legally permissible transfers from an original owner who acquired it justly. But nobody can claim to have made the natural world, and most ownership claims to land in the UK have been interrupted by discontinuities when the land has been allocated by force, state decree or conquest.

Ownership of the natural world has been justified by a series of post-hoc rationalisations, but in reality has 'stolen imperceptibly upon the world' (Thomas Paine 1797a: 6).

Historical claims

This reliance on past historical claims, based either in violent conquest or the arbitrary decisions of rulers, is a deeply unsatisfactory way of resolving the question of who has the right to territory, whether this is the right of an individual or of a state. It creates uncertainty (how far back historically do we trace the claims?) and leaves the way open to the use of force as a continuing way of settling disputes.

A historical basis for claims to land ownership also stokes up intergenerational conflict. Like a player joining a game of Monopoly that is in full swing, young people usually only have the chance to participate in the game as a landowner if another player gifts them some land on leaving the game.

Efficiency

Land use

In an ownership economy there is no cost of holding land, even if this is held out of use and derelict. There is an opportunity cost, the amount that is lost by not putting it to best use, but this is often less than the increase in the sale price (market value) of the land. This means that, while some people are in real need of land for housing or business, others are underusing land or holding it out of use.

Taxation

Orthodox taxes (apart from property taxes) fail to tax the market rent of land and so they fall on production, consumption and work. This discourages these economic activities and creates a Deadweight Loss that damages the economy.

The orthodox system of taxation creates further underuse of land. Orthodox taxes fall just as much on businesses in poor parts of the country as they do on areas where business is more profitable and in the more marginal areas this drives firms out of business.

The benefits system

In a complex economy it is rarely clear how much value each person contributes to the whole product of the economy. Sharing this out according to wages for work and interest on capital produces an arbitrary and unequal distribution of income. Many people are unable to work (youth, old age, sickness, unemployment ...) and so need to receive benefits from society as a whole. Because this requires taxation to provide a source of revenue, and because this taxation damages the economy, most states provide benefits that are mean and are conditional (on, for example, age, sickness, unemployment) and humiliating to recipients. Their design, particularly the unemployment and poverty traps, ensure that it is difficult for the poor to get in to work, further damaging the economy.

Land and natural resources are not the only government-granted monopolies that benefit one part of the population but not the rest, though they are the most outrageous because the resources are freely provided by nature and are essential to sustain life. In a similar way, other monopolies such as the right to create money, intellectual property rights and franchises for transport and utilities have been gifted by government to those they favour.

Stewardship

Stewardship is a form of private property that is held by individuals, corporations, groups of commoners and by states. In a stewardship economy the land is held in Trust for the benefit of everybody. A steward who claims the right to a plot of land has the present duty to pay stewardship fees that compensate others for excluding them from that land.

The environment is also held in Trust. Where a resource is used by a group of people small enough to reach agreement about its use, it is managed by agreement as a common pool resource. Where it is used by a large number of people, its use is allocated to whoever bids the highest amount for use-right permits and the revenue invested for the benefit of future generations or distributed as an Environmental Dividend.

Ethics

Stewardship has an ethical foundation that is at least as secure as that of ownership. It reduces the potential for conflict between states, between individuals and between generations.

Stewardship Economy accepts the conventional justification for the ownership of artefacts, the things that we humans make. But it rejects the special rights-based arguments that ownership rights in land can be based on first occupancy or the first mixing of labour. It does not advocate common or collective ownership in place of private ownership. It goes further and rejects the claim that it is possible to base a claim of ownership on any historical act.

Stewardship proposes that property rights should take a new form that is conditional on both the formal responsibility to care for that land and the formal duty to pay a ground rent, equal to its market rent, to the wider community. This requirement for an ongoing payment turns the liberal conception of ownership, perpetual and unconditional, into a conditional use-right. It turns land from a financial asset into an earth community of which we are members (Jonty Williams 2014: 26).

Stewardship may be justified from a variety of political or philosophical positions.. Socialists follow Karl Marx in believing that the land should really be nationalised, and the rents used for the common purpose. Left-libertarians follow Henry George in drawing on Natural Law, or Hillel Steiner in his argument from self-ownership. Liberals who want to reconcile social with economic liberalism follow the arguments of Gavin Kerr (2017).

Stewardship Economy takes a different approach in that it does not seek to justify stewardship from any chosen philosophical position. Rather it examines each of the duties, rights and goals that have been proposed as justifications for ownership and suggests that they provide an equal or greater justification for stewardship. The exceptions of course are the special rights of first occupancy and labour and having dismissed these as unconvincing in a world where 'as much and as good' is *not* available to the landless it proposes an alternative special right – the special right derived from compensating all those who are excluded from that land.

Conditionality on paying the ground rent means that there is no need to resort to adjudicating between competing historical claims. Property rights can be determined in the present between individuals and between states. This removes the potential for conflict between states that accept the principle of stewardship and provides a mechanism for its resolution where it arises.

The nature of the relationship of the steward with their neighbours changes with the payment of stewardship fees. Instead of depending for the security of their borders on legal claims backed up by the police they can rest assured that their neighbours far and wide are properly compensated for the steward's exclusive use of that land. Property rights are consensual or, as Jonty Williams puts it, hospitable (Jonty Williams 2014: 12).

Determining property rights in the present also puts recent generations on an equal footing with earlier generations, removing a major source of inter-generational conflict.

Efficiency

A stewardship economy is far more efficient than an ownership economy in the way that land is used, in the functioning of the economy, in the impact of the benefit system on employment, in the delivery of benefits and in the management of the environment. It provides an efficient way to handle government investment in infrastructure and other public goods; and an efficient way to manage state-created monopolies such as the creation of money, transport networks, utilities and intellectual property rights.

Land use

The steward of land pays a market rent for their land, just as a tenant does today in an ownership economy. Very few people in this position would continue to pay rent if they were making little or no use of their land. In a stewardship economy there would be little or no empty homes, derelict land, land underused by speculators or land banking.

Many landlords would continue to rent their land to tenants, particularly where they own significant improvements such as blocks of flats – and where they are also providing a valuable social and economic function. But many others would be likely to sell to their tenants. As a result, more land would be cared for by stewards directly, and this would be likely to lead to better use of the land.

Taxation

Stewardship fees can be described as a fee or a charge, but they are not strictly speaking a tax as their purpose is to allocate land efficiently not to raise revenue for the government. This is why the term 'stewardship fees' is more satisfactory than 'Land Value Tax'. They can, however, be compared with conventional taxes and are clearly more efficient – they create no deadweight loss and allocate land more efficiently.

The principle of stewardship is that the revenue from these ground rents is used in two ways. Part of it is paid to the whole population on an equal per capita basis as a Universal Income. And part is paid to the government, replacing all taxation other than that which is in place to effect behaviour change such as taxes on tobacco, alcohol, plastic bags and carbon.

124

The efficiency of stewardship fees compared with orthodox taxes is unarguable, even amongst orthodox economists trained in a discipline that conflates land with capital in its models. Orthodox taxation imposes a Deadweight Loss on an economy that can only be estimated but probably amounts to at least 20% of GDP, or £2000 per man, woman and child in the UK. Substituting stewardship fees for orthodox taxes would provide a major boost to the economy.

Universal Income

A Universal Income, adequately funded in a stewardship economy, is far more efficient than the conditional benefit systems with which we are familiar in ownership economies. It achieves a high uptake and is cheap to deliver. It encourages people to work, particularly where all that is available is part-time and low-paid work, in ways that are flexible and fit in with the other commitments they have in life. This small private income enables people to care for others, take part in education and re-skilling, take entrepreneurial risks and to engage in a wide range of creative activity that does not guarantee an income in the market but that contributes greatly to our society and economy. And it does all this respectfully and equally.

Government-granted monopolies

Stewardship is completely compatible with monopolies such as transport networks and utilities being managed directly by the state. But where these are judged to be best managed by private or not-for-profit corporations monopoly rights are not given away to those the government favours for reasons that may be rational but may be corrupt. Instead, they are leased to whoever is prepared to meet the regulatory requirements *and* to pay the highest market rent for their use – as was achieved in the auctions for electromagnetic spectrum. This approach offers the possibility of these monopolies being managed by those best able to do so.

Tradable permits

Tradable permits are already widely accepted amongst economists and politicians as the most practical way to shape our behaviour towards the environment by ensuring that the price of things that cause environmental damage reflects their true costs, including those to society and the environment.

Permits for the use of the environment follow the same rationale as stewardship fees for land – anybody who uses the natural world owes everybody else compensation equal to the resource rent, the market rent of that asset.

Environmental Dividend

The legitimacy of asking people and firms to buy environmental permits for the use of renewable resources is assured by redistributing the revenue to everybody on an equal basis. We all get an equal share of the wealth of the natural world.

Investing for sustainability

When we reduce the stores of natural capital, either by depleting non-renewable resources or by irreversible pollution, the true cost of this damage is collected and invested for future generations.

Transition

Ethics

Where there are no established private property rights it would be feasible to introduce stewardship overnight at the full rate of 100 per cent of the ground rent. But in an ownership economy this would amount to confiscation of the ownership rights and asset values held by landowners. This would be difficult to justify as these landowners have operated according to the laws of the land, and this risks penalising them unfairly. Some argue that landowners have, often for generations, benefited from an inherently unfair regime of property rights and that rather than being spared these penalties they should be asked to repay the rent that they have failed to share. But most people would want to find a route for transition to stewardship that feels fair even to those who currently own land.

Making a gradual transition over, say, ten years is a fudge that will continue to feel unfair to those who have to pay. The transition described here accepts that people should keep the assets, that is to say the price of the land that they have acquired legally, but that a tax of 100 per cent should be levied on any future increase in the market rent of that land. This may seem too harsh for many landowners and too generous for many reformers.

Efficiency

This proposed transition mechanism is not as efficient as a rapid transition in which the full market rent is paid, but it is probably as efficient as can be achieved by political agreement in a democratic country with established property rights.

Taxing only the increase in the market rent of land produces one unexpected advantage over taxing a gradually increasing proportion of the total market rent of the land. It puts an immediate cap on the market value (sale price) of land. This means that from Day 1 there is a complete end to speculation in land, and even to the speculative element that makes owning land so beneficial compared with renting. People would immediately lose the financial incentive to 'get on the housing ladder' (even if the incentive to own one's own place and take responsibility for the state of its upkeep remains). This would result in an immediate increase in the amount of land and landed property on the market. And the immediate introduction of the New Land Market with its sale by auction would increase the efficiency of transferring property. All this would take place before any market rent had actually been paid.

There are practical proposals for transition that would not be unduly disruptive. National Non-Domestic (Business) Rates in the UK raise about the right amount of revenue from business land but suffer from a number of disadvantages that damage business. The revaluations are infrequent and do not reflect the actual market rents paid for business land; the basis of valuation is the market value of the land in its current rather than its highest and best use; there are numerous exceptions that are subsidised by the businesses that do pay their rates, most seriously for derelict and for agricultural land; and the rates penalise those who develop and make good use of their land while subsidising those who fail to improve it (Julian Pratt 2014: 1).

There are political parties that support at least the exploration of replacing National Non-Domestic (Business) Rates by a Land Value Tax – in the 2017 election this was an explicit manifesto promise of the Labour party, and Land Value Taxation was supported in principle by the Liberal Democrats and Green parties.

Once Land Value Taxation has been introduced for business land many of the main objections, particularly those related to valuation, will be seen to be of minor significance, and the replacement of Council Tax by a Land Value Tax will become a more straightforward political proposition.

In conclusion

Ownership of artefacts - the things that people make is justified by the history of voluntary transactions that lead back to the original maker.

Ownership of land and the rest of the natural world has at best 'stolen imperceptibly upon the world' and at worst has been the result of theft by the powerful from the weak. John Locke's view that ownership of land is justified by 'mixing one's labour' with the land confuses the ownership of improvements - artefacts that should indeed be the property of their creator - with that of the land itself. His view that it is justified by 'first occupation' could only possibly hold in conditions where 'as much and as good' is left for others, a situation that has probably never held and certainly does not do so today.

These beliefs have allowed states, individuals and corporations to acquire land by power and coercion and have divided populations into payers and receivers of rent. The receivers of rent have become progressively richer while the payers of rent have never earned more than the bare minimum to keep them alive and prevent them from rebelling against the landowners. Even the owners of capital have only received the return that they could expect from investing in the least productive sites.

Where the state has itself claimed ownership of land, this has given the state power over its citizens which it has consolidated by patronage. Where private individuals have claimed ownership of land, they have extracted rent from their fellow-citizens and passed it on to their heirs.

The attractiveness of land as a financial asset has made it unavailable to many who want to put it to use as a home or for business. The capture of rent by landowners has deprived states of their natural source of revenue and driven them to levy taxes on production and consumption which damage the economy and further impoverish the landless.

We can do better than that. We need to recognise that ownership of the natural world cannot arise from a historical claim and instead stewardship of the natural world needs to be conditional on caring for the land and on paying ground rent, the market rent of the land, to the wider community.

Global peace and prosperity is not an impossible dream if we understand our proper relationship with the Earth.